Beauty

Off-duty

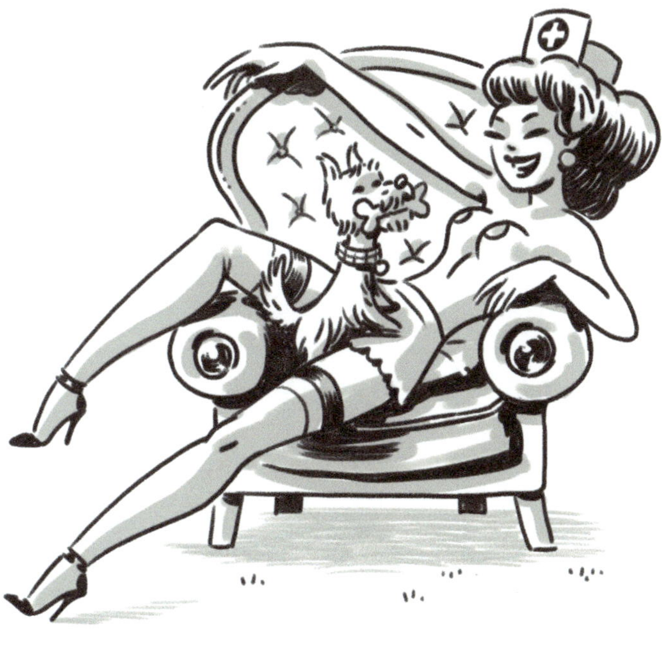

Published in 2019 by Wolfbait Books

www.wolfbait.co.uk

ISBN: 978-1-9162151-0-8

A catalogue record of this book is available at the British Library.

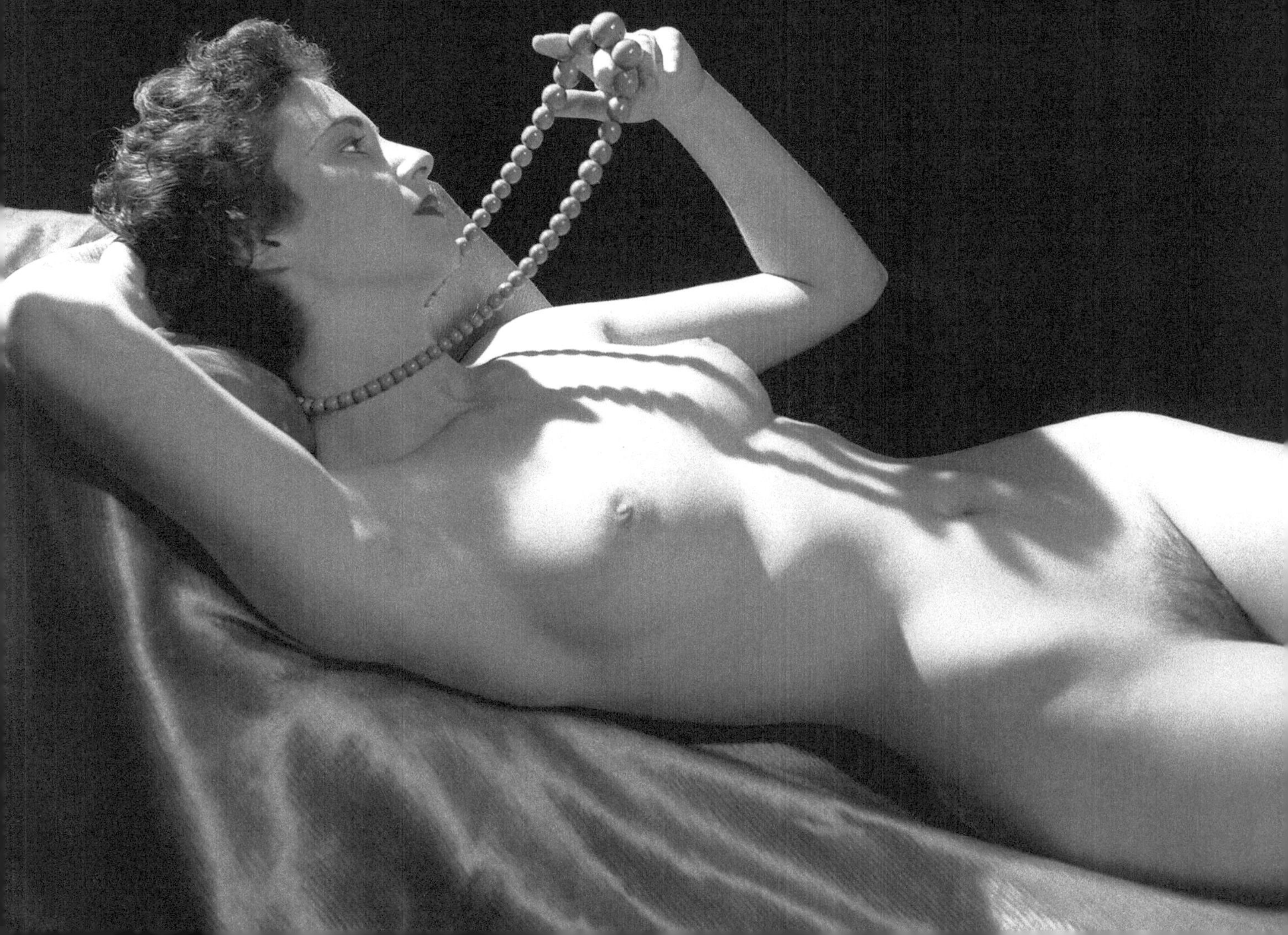

Beauty

Off-duty

By Yahya El-Droubie

Photography by Stephen Glass

Illustrations by Colin Gordon

WOLFBAIT

UNDER THE COUNTER CULTURE

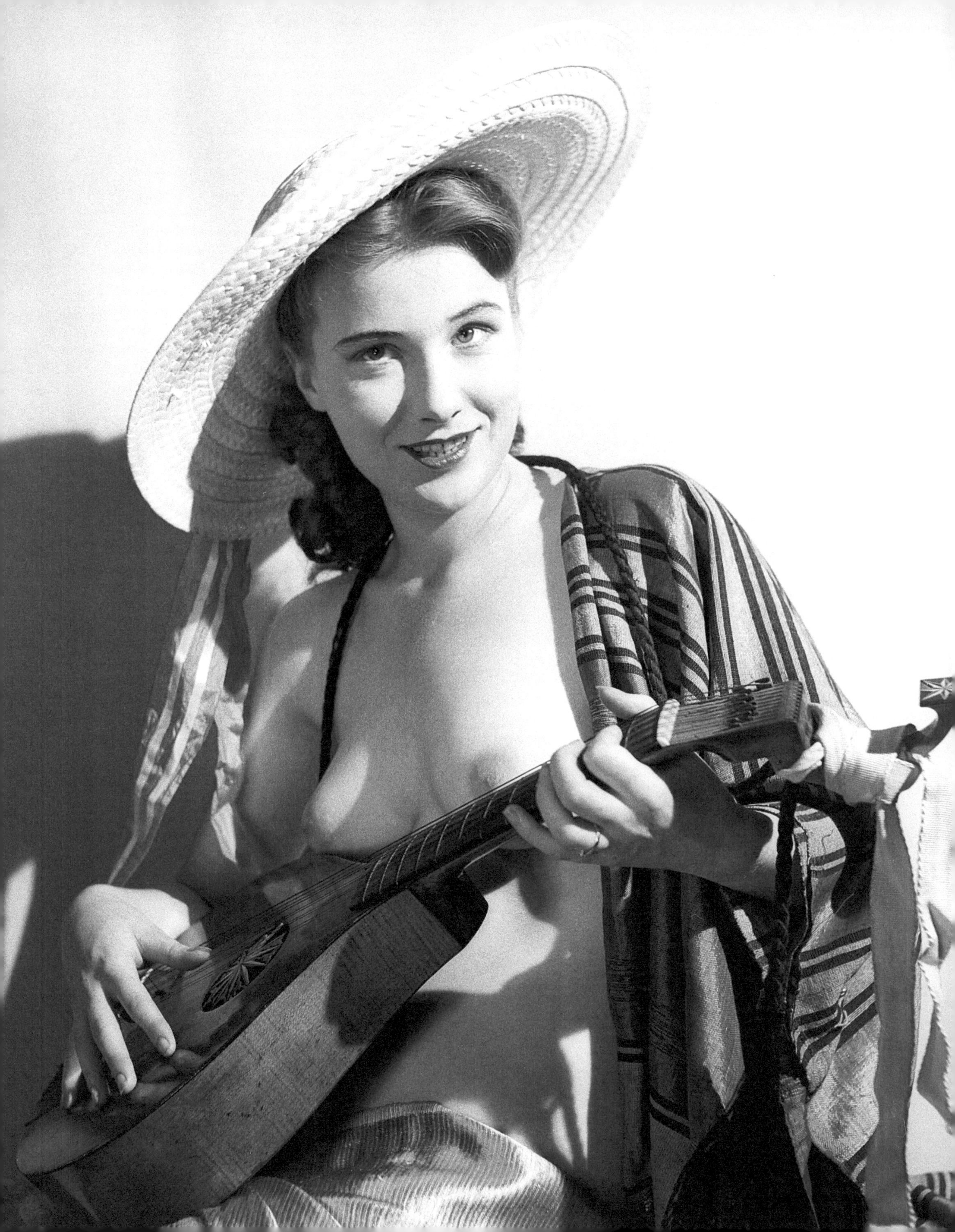

Introduction

THE PHOTOGRAPHER STEPHEN GLASS is something of an enigma. He was sufficiently well-known during the 1950s for his name to be prominently displayed on magazine covers to help sell them, but very little was written about him or his work at that time. The opposite is true of his elder brother, Zoltán, who was also a photographer. Known to his friends as "Zolly", Zoltán was featured and interviewed in numerous magazines on both sides of the Atlantic.

The beauty of the human figure is, and always has been, despite intervals of prudery, a source of inspiration.
– Walter Bird A.R.P.S.

Zoltán Glass was born in Budapest, Hungary, on April 26, 1903. He began his career as a cartoonist and retoucher for a local newspaper, but in 1925 he moved to Berlin, where he was employed as the picture editor of an evening newspaper; he then moved on to the *Berliner Tagblatt* as a photojournalist. Zoltán prospered and was soon able to develop a thriving freelance business as a commercial photographer and journalist. He established Reclaphot, a photographic agency that specialised in advertising work, and Autophot, a company dedicated exclusively to automobile photography. A keen motor sport enthusiast and amateur racer, Zoltán covered Germany's biggest races at the Nürburgring and Avus circuits. His famous photographs are of the Mercedes-Benz Silver Arrows team, which dominated Grand Prix racing in the mid-1930s.

With the rise of Hitler, business became increasingly difficult in Germany, and Zoltán fled to London. As an enemy alien at the outbreak of World War II, he was not permitted to pursue his profession and faced the threat of internment, so he voluntarily handed over his camera equipment to the British authorities.

After the war, Zoltán eked out a living taking publicity stills for clients in the film and theatre worlds. His career took a big step up when fellow Hungarian Arpad Elfer, Creative Director of Colman, Prentis & Varley, one of the most prestigious London ad agencies, started giving him work. By the mid-1950s, he was one of the most successful fashion and advertising photographers in the capital, with a studio at 183 Kings Road, Chelsea, and later another at 41 Paradise Walk, SW3.

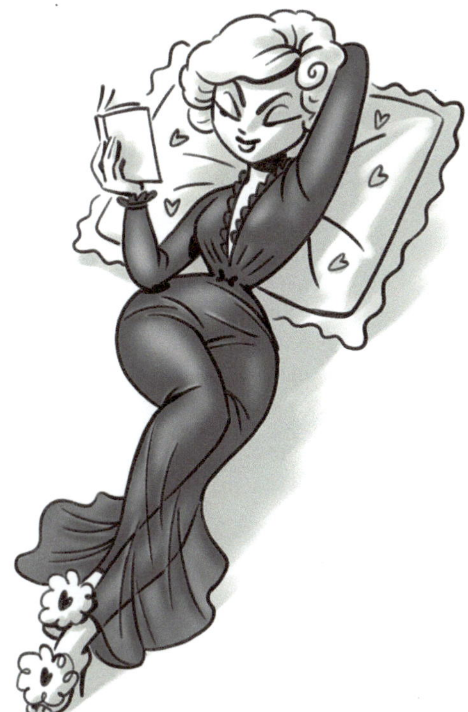

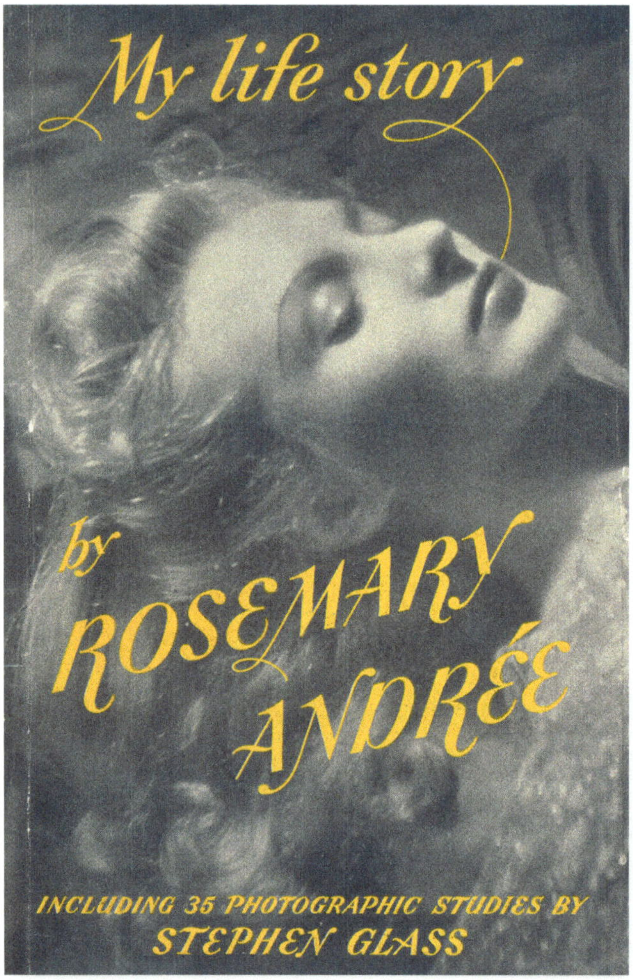

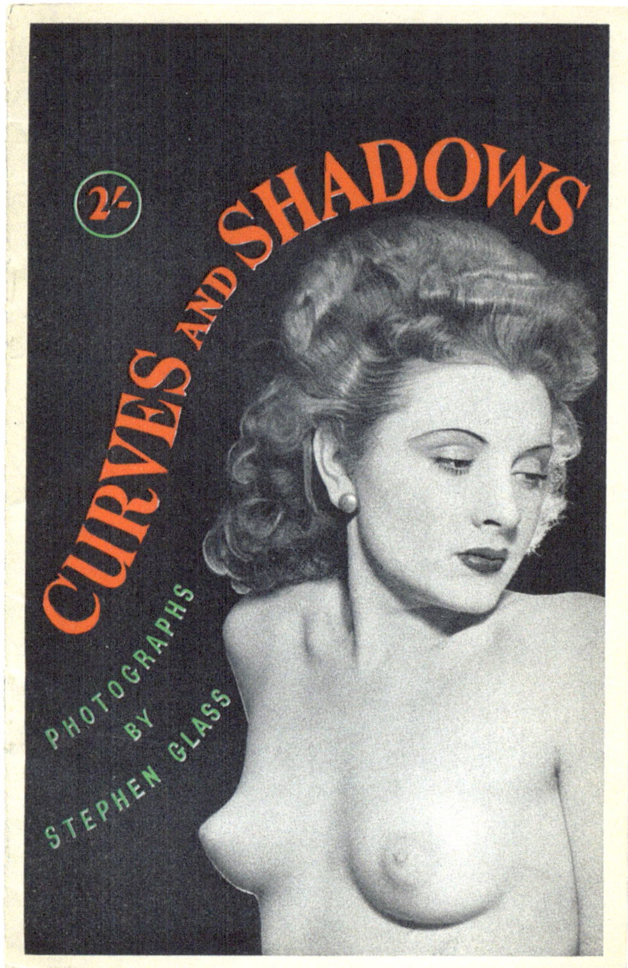

Above left: *My Life Story* by Rosemary Andrée, with an art supplement by Stephen Glass, published by The Naturist Ltd., 1945. Rosemary Andrée was a popular dancer and body culture enthusiast who found fame in the 1930s with her acrobatic dance routines with Jimmy Gaston. As a proponent of the benefits of exercise, she was happy to pose nude for photographers such as Stephen Glass and Walter Bird and became known as "The English Venus".

Above right: *Curves and Shadows,* published by Gnome Publications, Covent Garden, London. Fourteen black and white images including the cover, circa 1955.

One of his clients was Odhams Press, who published *Lilliput*, a pocket-sized gentleman's magazine that featured an assortment of titillating articles and risqué humour, together with adventurous photographic essays from such well-known talents as Bill Brandt and Brassai.

Zoltán's brother, Stephen, who also fled Europe during World War II, carved out a name for himself taking pictures for such publications as *The Naturist* and *Health and Efficiency.* The well-known model Pamela Green (1929–2010) posed for him several times at the infamous nudist camp Spielplatz in Bricket Wood, Hertfordshire, and at his tiny first-floor studio in Old Church Street, just off the Kings Road in Chelsea. *"In those days, when Stephen photographed me, I still had dark hair. He liked his props, especially stuffed animals,"* she said. Pamela's agent, Pearl Beresford, sent her along to Zoltán, whose studio on the Kings Road was enormous by comparison. Unlike Stephen, Zoltán was brisk and businesslike.

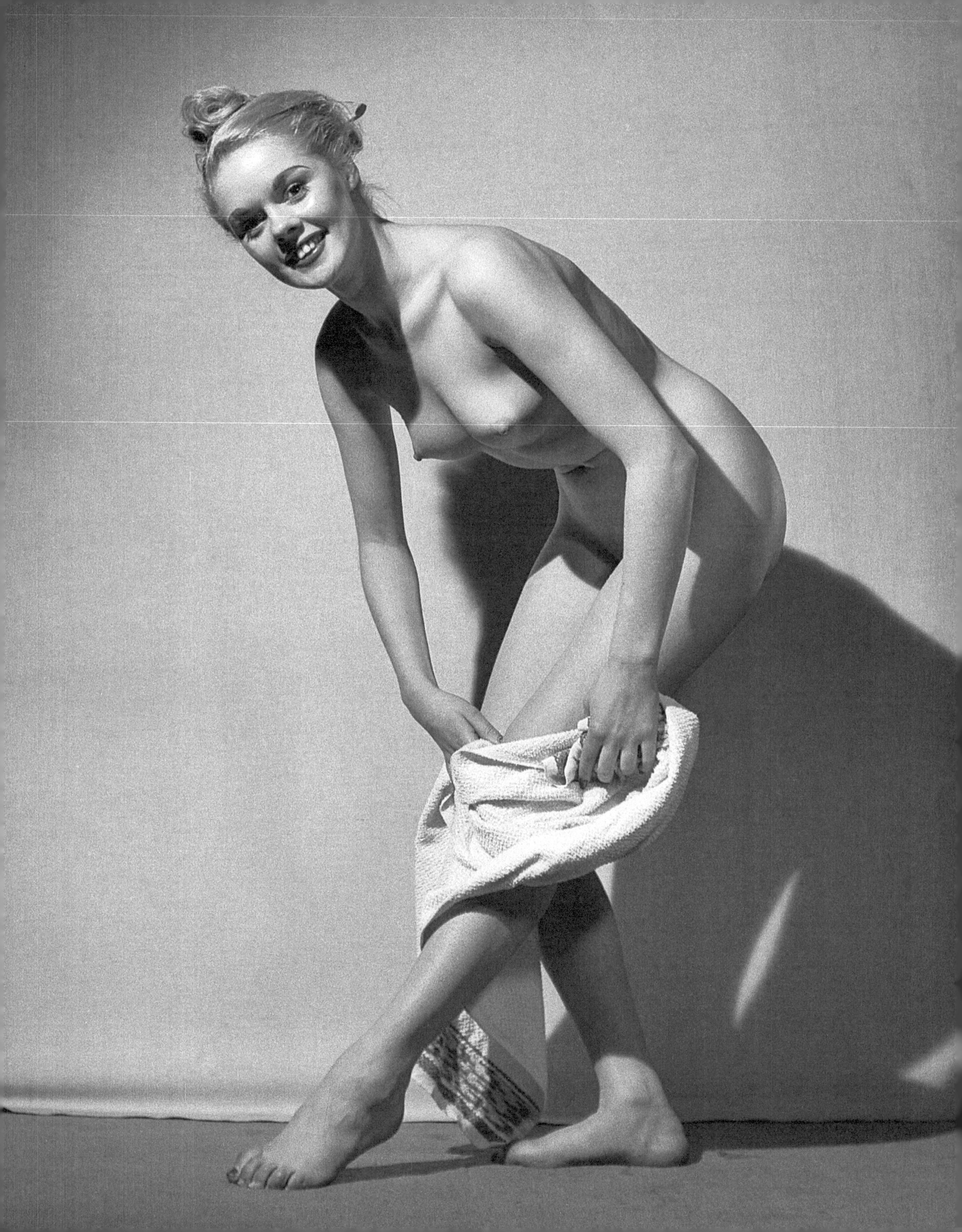

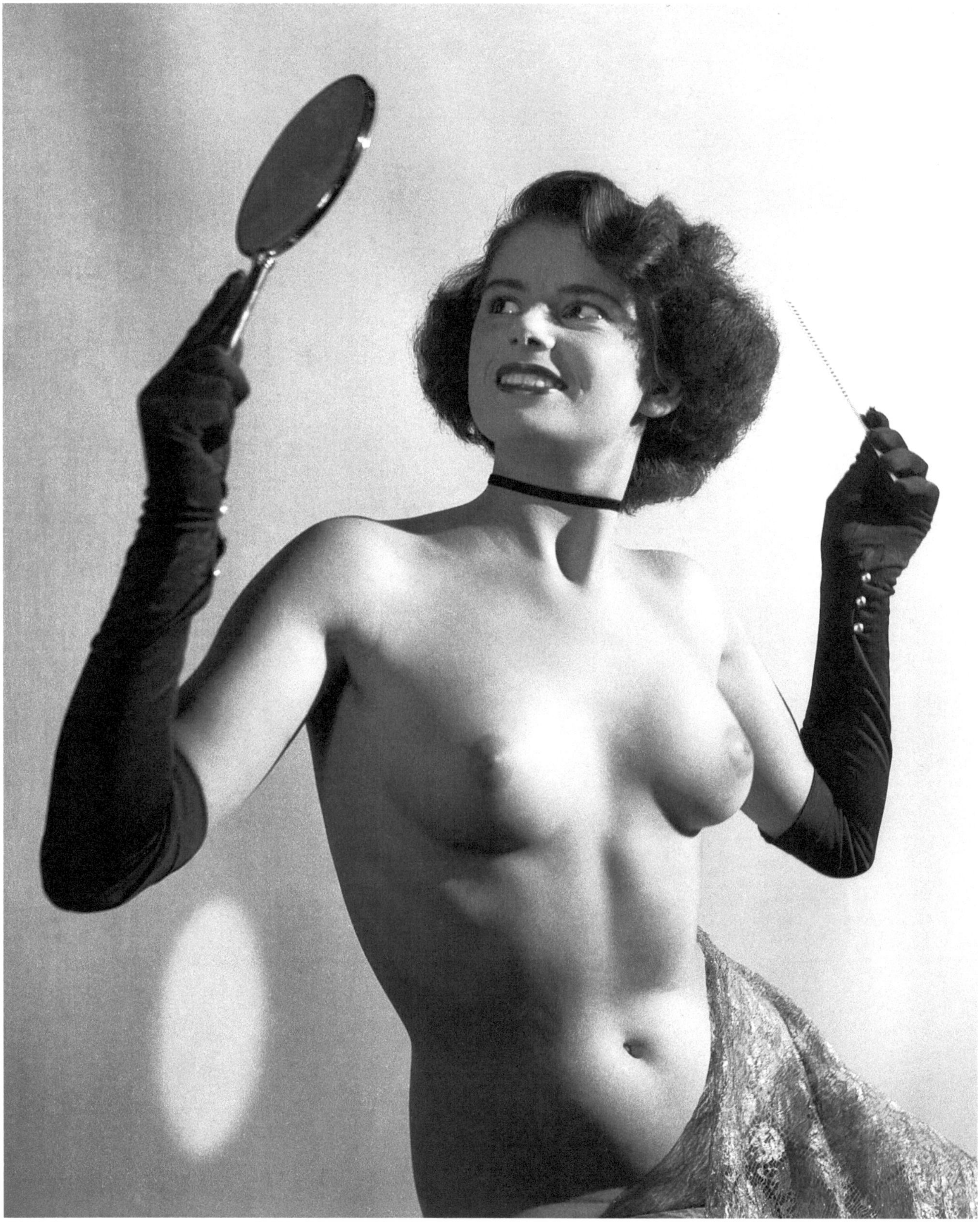

Iseult, the daughter of Spielplatz co-founders Charles and Dorothy Macaskie, remembers Stephen. *"He would often ask me to pose for him,"* she said. *"I quite enjoyed having my photo taken, but when I asked to be paid, he stopped using me. A bit of pocket money back then would have been nice."*

As well as magazines, Stephen's work graced a series of small books published by The Naturist Ltd., such as *Sussex Maidens* (1949), *The Pool of Enchantment* (1950) and *Nudist Life in Spielplatz* (1956). He also photographed the popular model June Palmer (1940–2004). The photos in this book are from his uncensored negatives.

Until the end of the 1960s, it was considered obscene to show pubic hair or genitalia in British publications. To ensure an image of a naked young lady would not incur the wrath of the censor, the model would shave down below and the photograph would then be retouched by hand to erase anything problematic.

By 1964, Zoltán Glass had made enough money to sell his Chelsea studios to a consortium of British photographers. He then moved to a villa in Roquebrune on the French Riviera, with his common-law wife Pat, a former cabaret dancer. He offered his collection of pin-up photography to glamour photographer Harrison Marks who, strangely, turned it down. Zoltán died in France on February 24, 1981, at the age of 78, leaving neither offspring nor a will. His photographs were eventually given to The National Science and Media Museum in Bradford, Yorkshire. Stephen Glass died on 23 April, 1990. His work ended up at auction.

Today women have conquered freedom to serve as an inspiration to art without any moral damage. For some inexplicable reason, many artists do not avail themselves of the wealth of willing models. A phenomenal and strange thing that escapes comprehension.

– B. Fotherington-Tomas

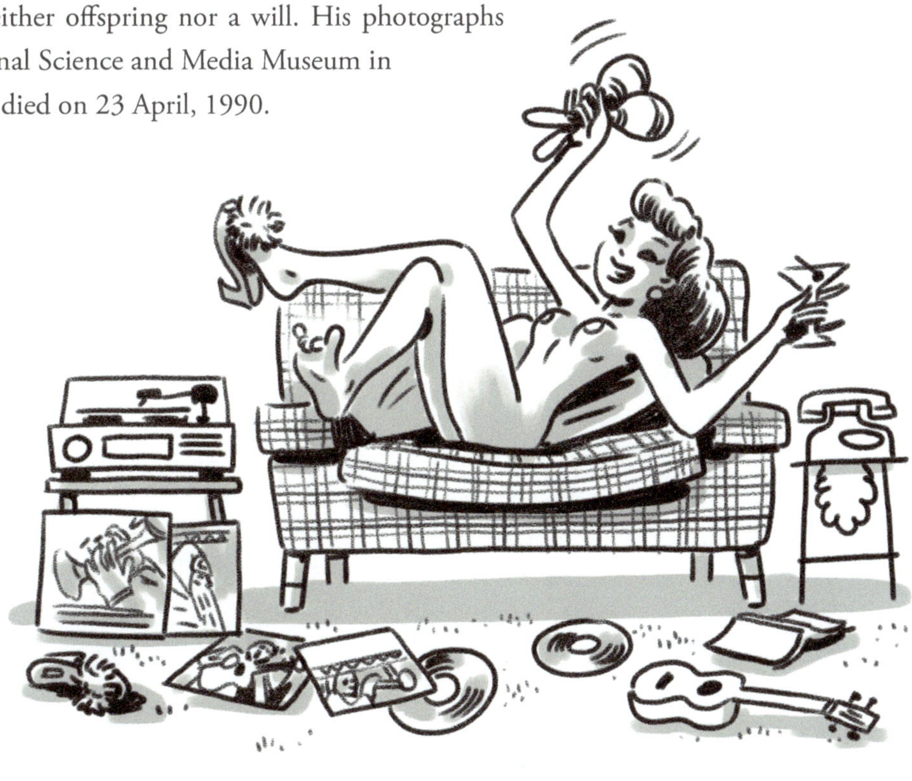

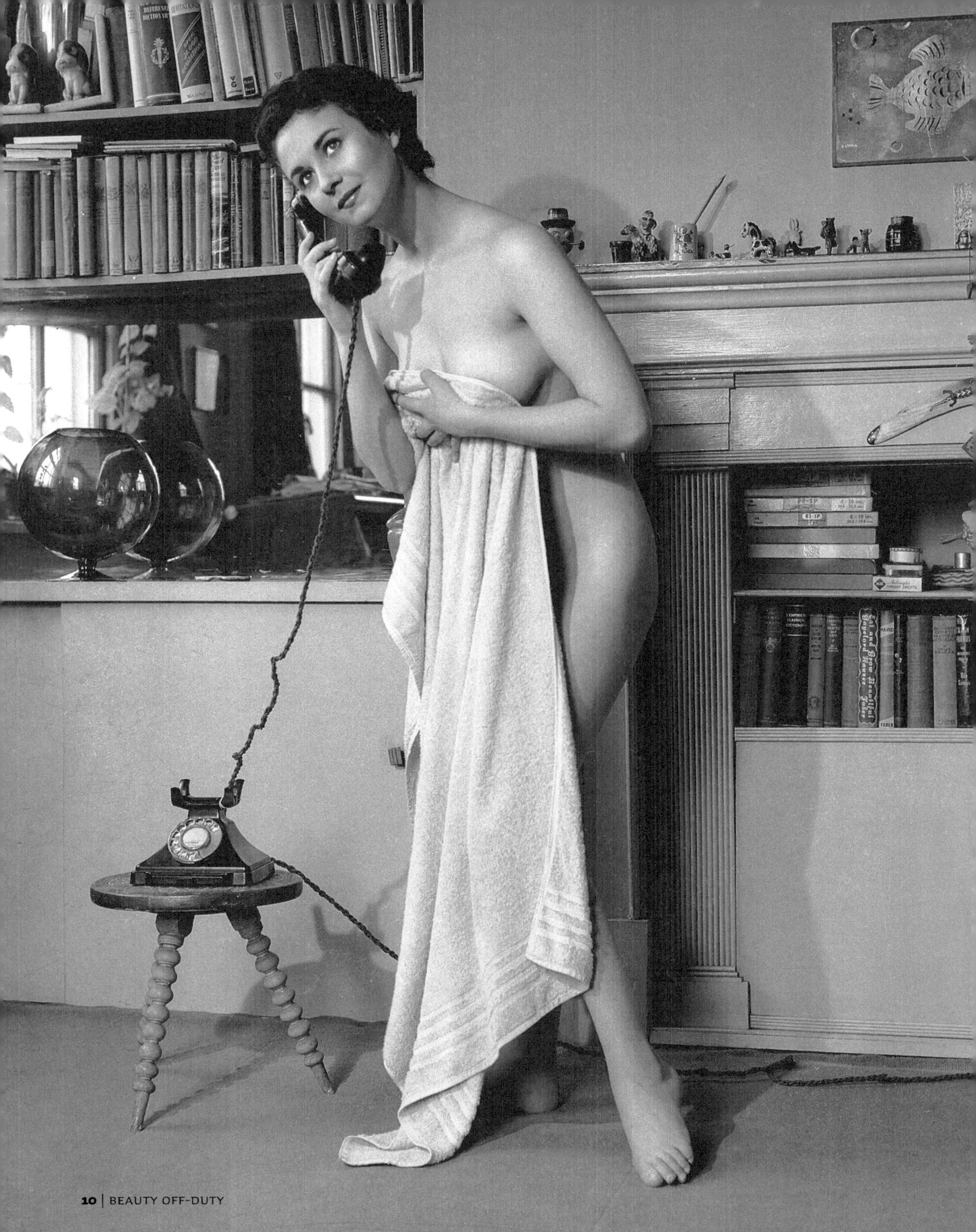

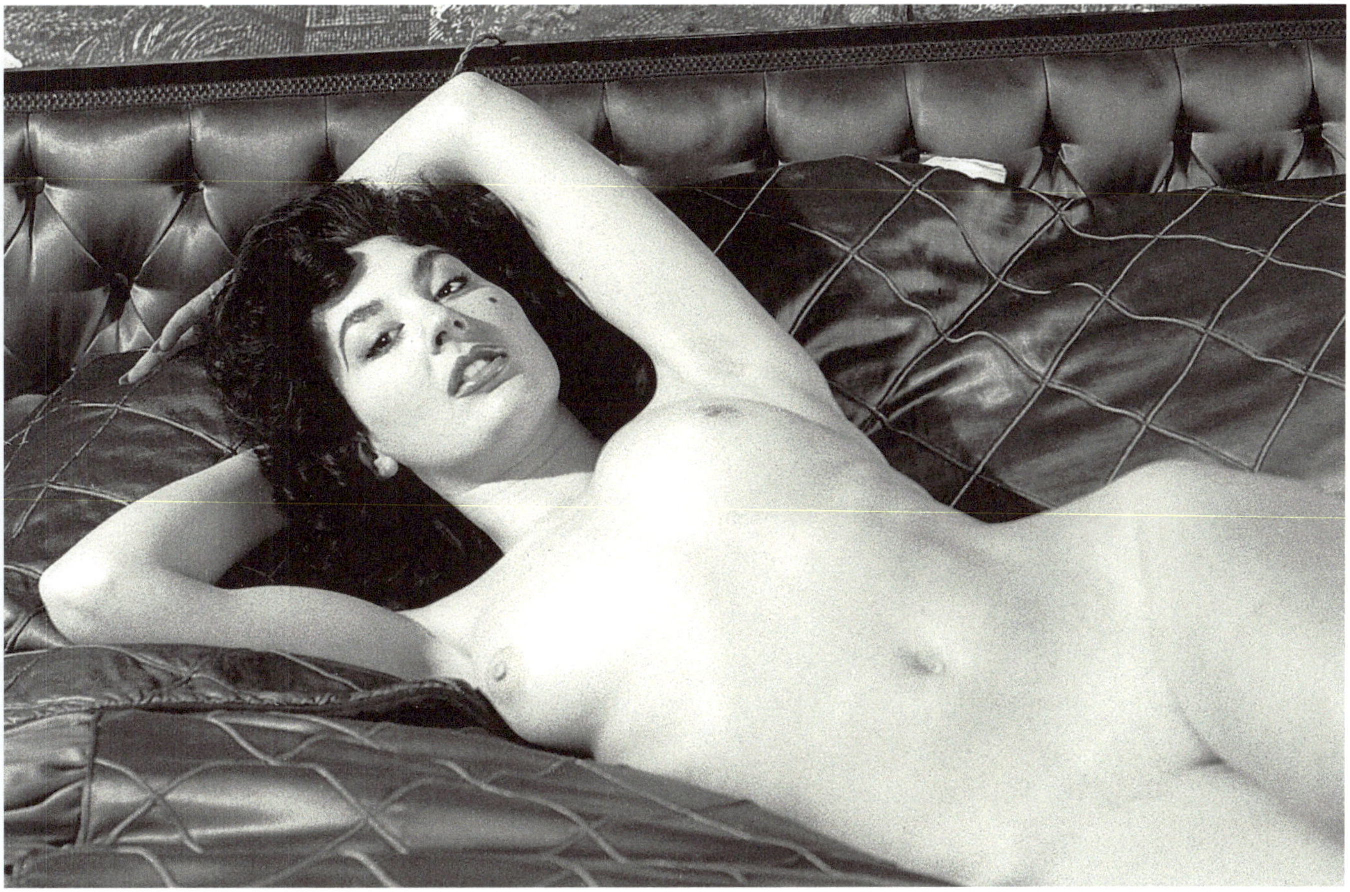

Glamour girls are mostly photographed in the studio or some exotic location, so one often wonders what they look like relaxing at home. Wolfbait is devoted to showing you just that. And as you will see, these girls, whether on the phone, getting dressed, doing a bit of DIY or just hanging out nude on a hot day by the fireplace, are just as lovely for it. Sure it's not their home — it's most likely Stephen Glass's flat in West London — but what's wrong with a little bit of make-believe? These "relaxed", everyday moments caught on camera tap into the phenomena of the "girl next door" so wonderfully exploited by *Playboy* when it first launched in 1953. Up till then men's magazines, especially in the US, were dominated by buxom, pneumatic strippers such as Tempest Storm and scary but alluring femme fatales. Even if you survived a date with them, they were not the kind of girl you would want to take home to meet your parents. The girls in the following pages, albeit professional models like Lee Sothern and Anita Smith, maintain the innocence and playful charm of the "girl next door" — credit must be given tothe lensman, Stephen Glass, for capturing it for our delectation.

There is no denying, landscapes, seascapes, fruit and flowers have charms of their own, but not these charms.

– D. Wolter

Above: Lee Sothern.

Far left: "Whitehall 1212,"Anita Smith

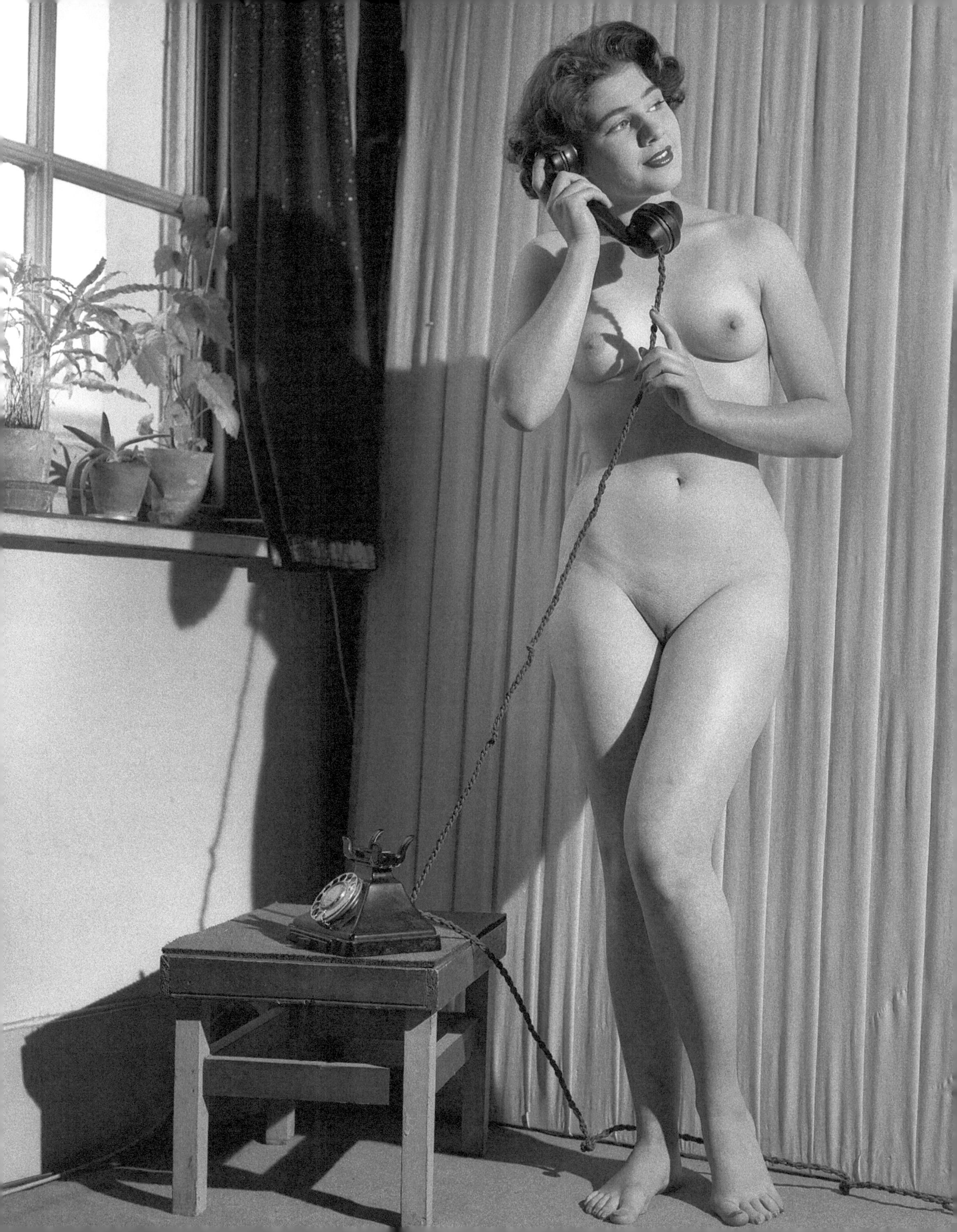

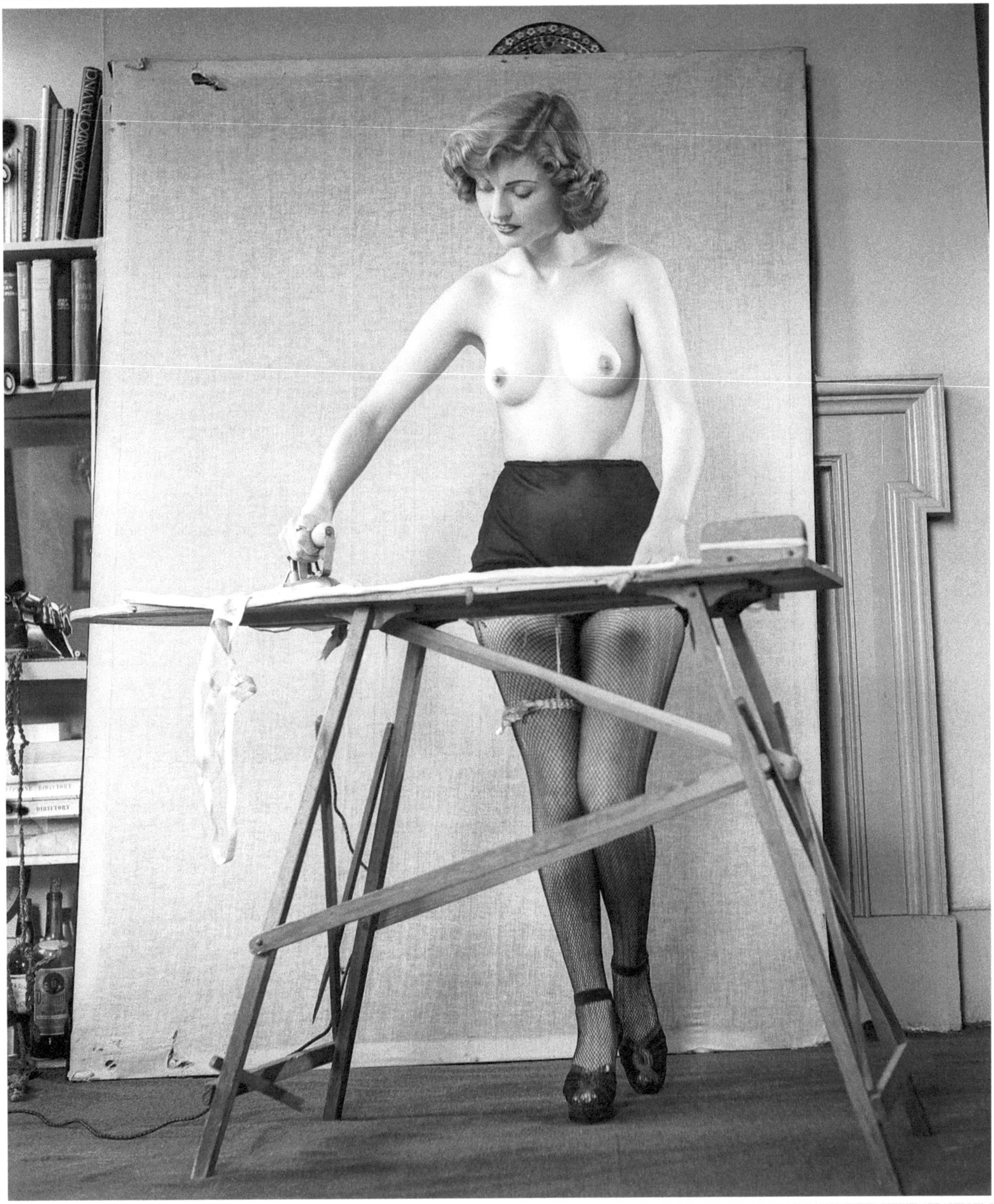

Left: Julie Alexander, a former receptionist from Fulham, London.

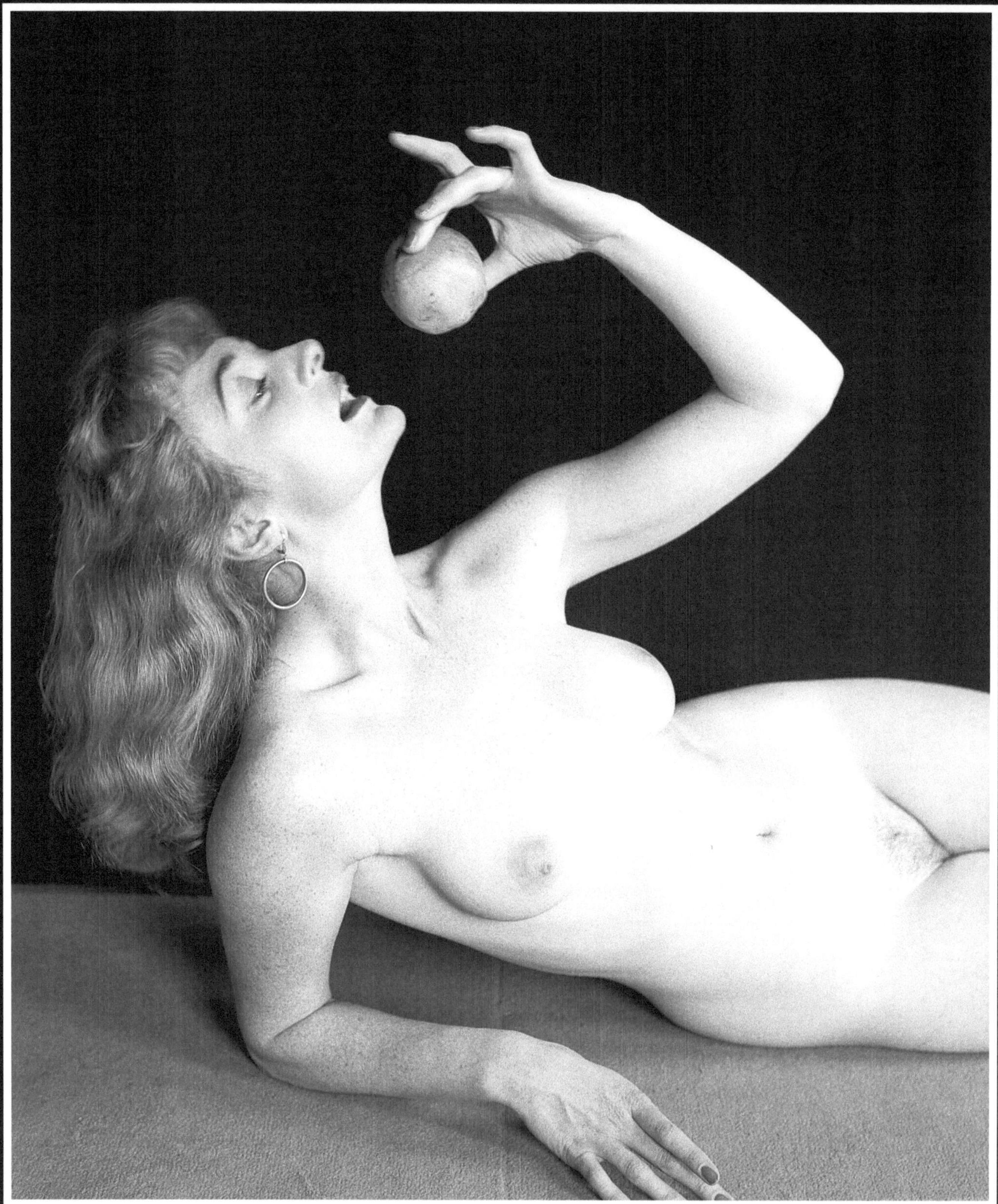

Above: Eve Harrison **Right:** Audrey Hill.

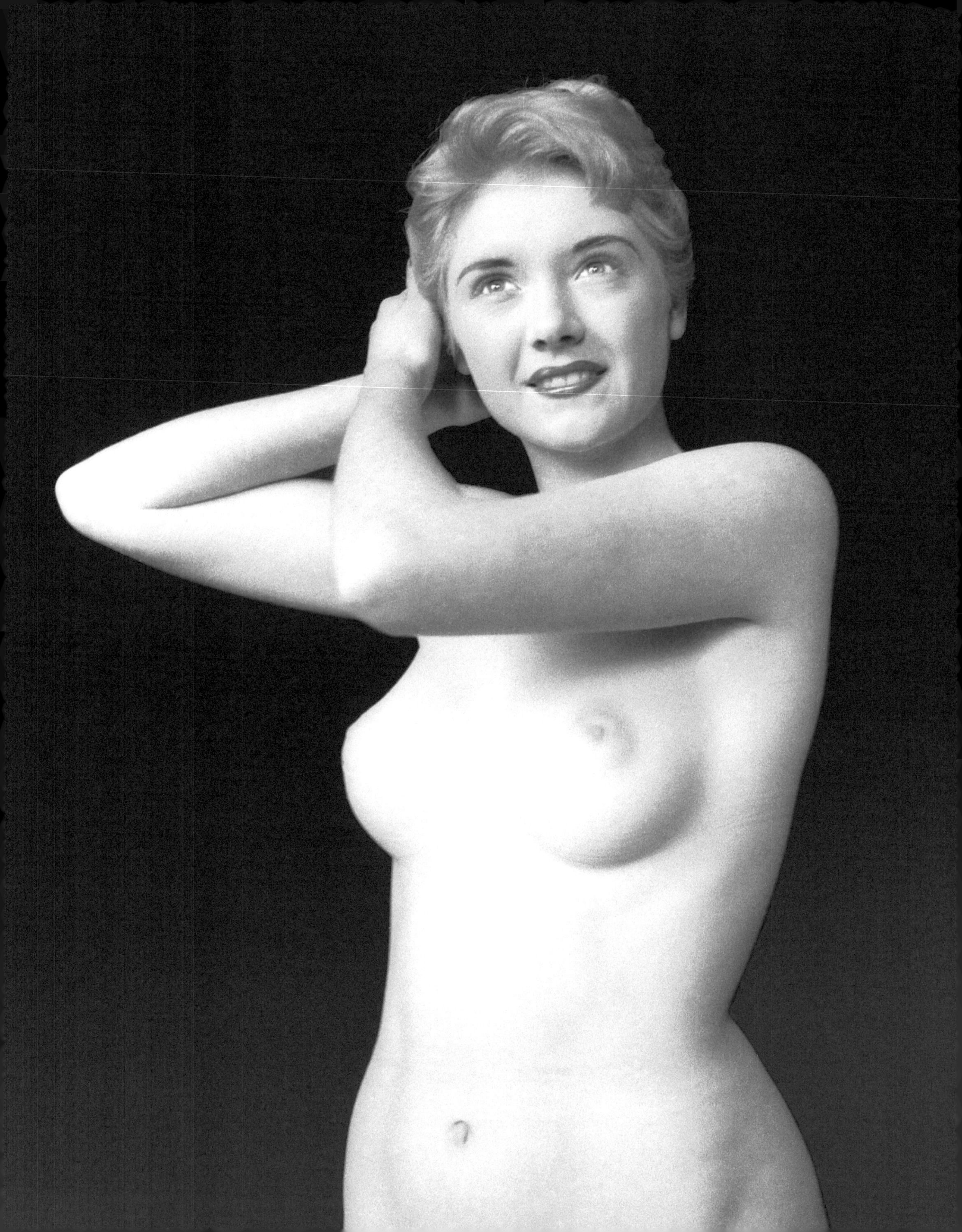

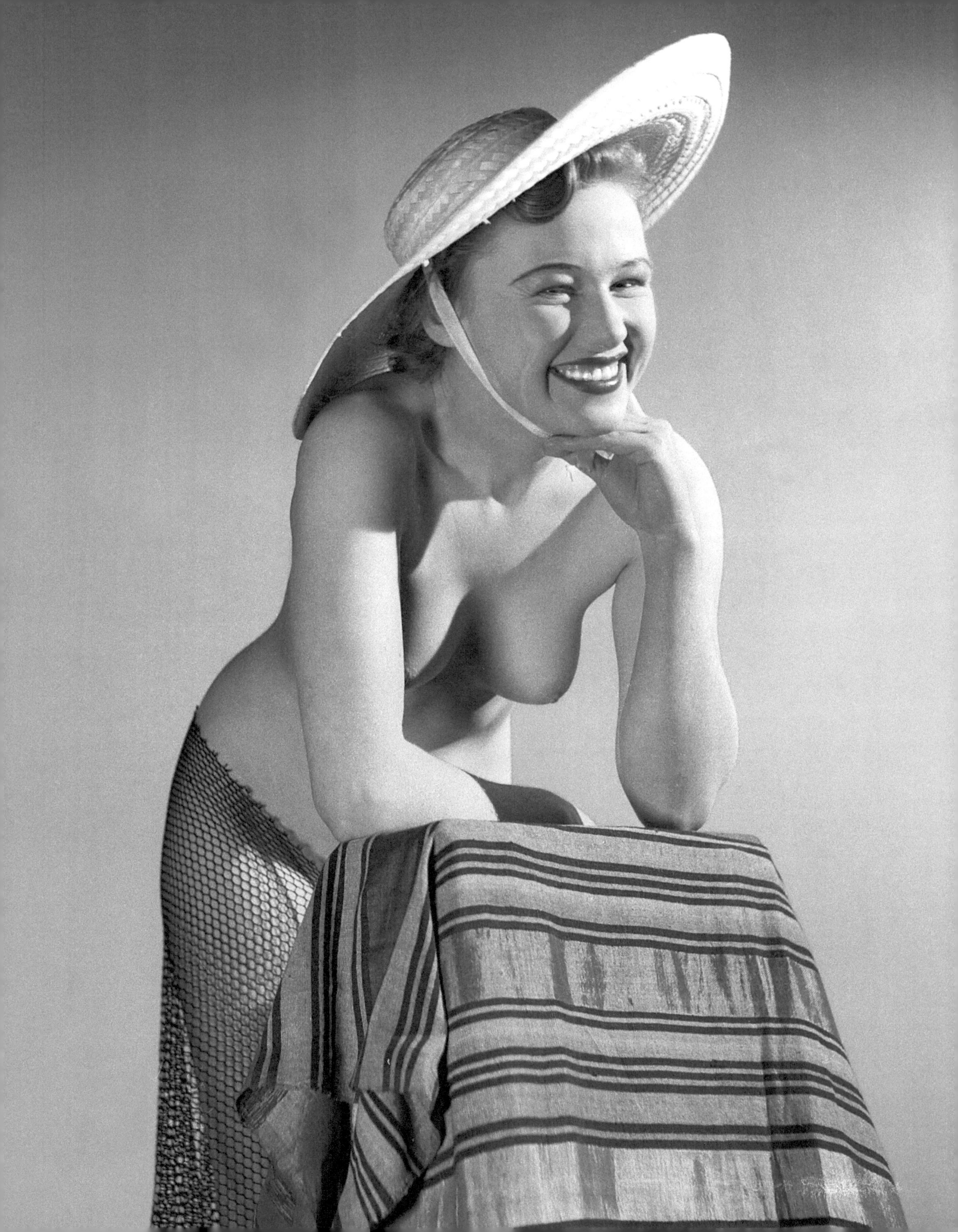

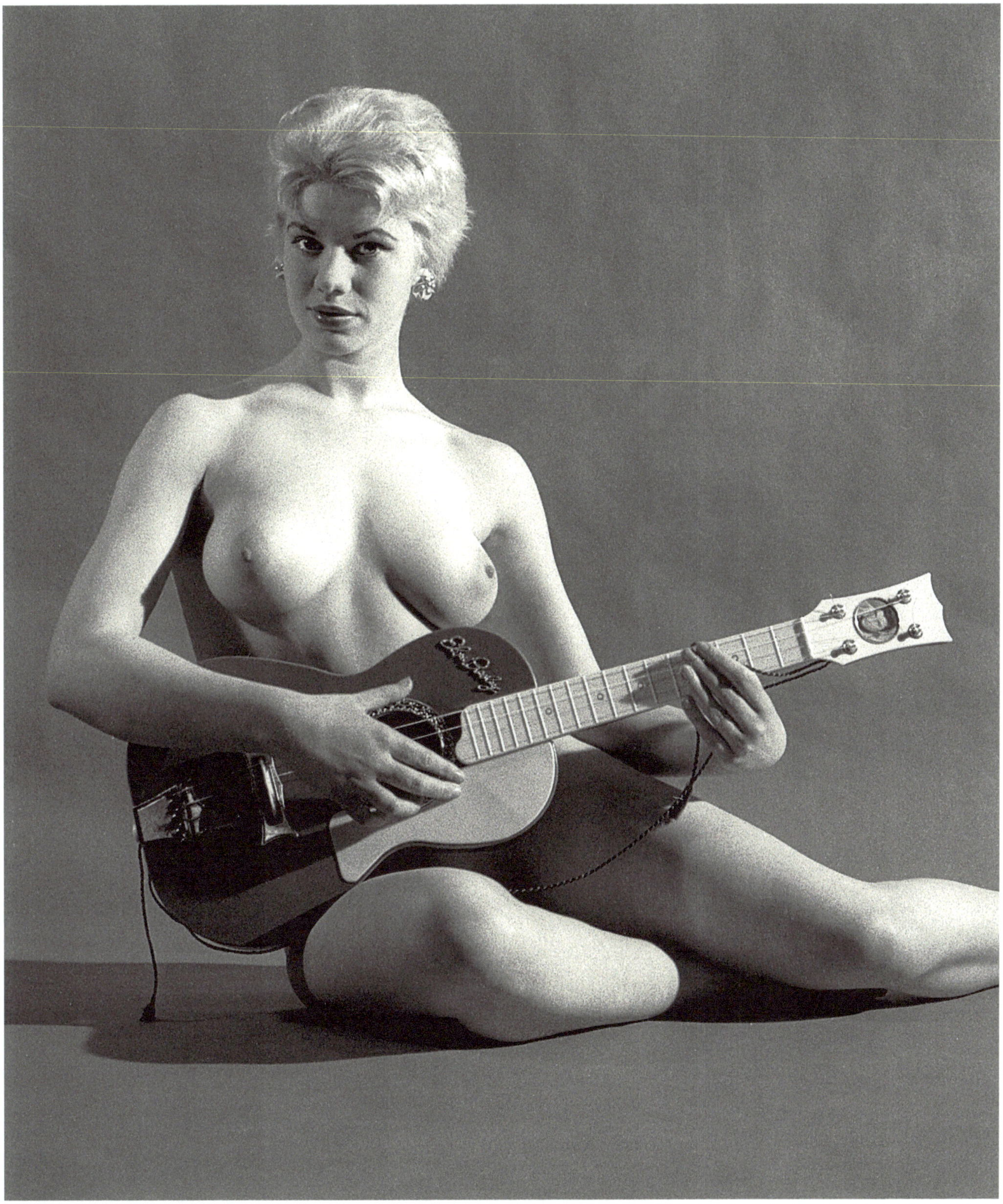

Above: Kim Foster.

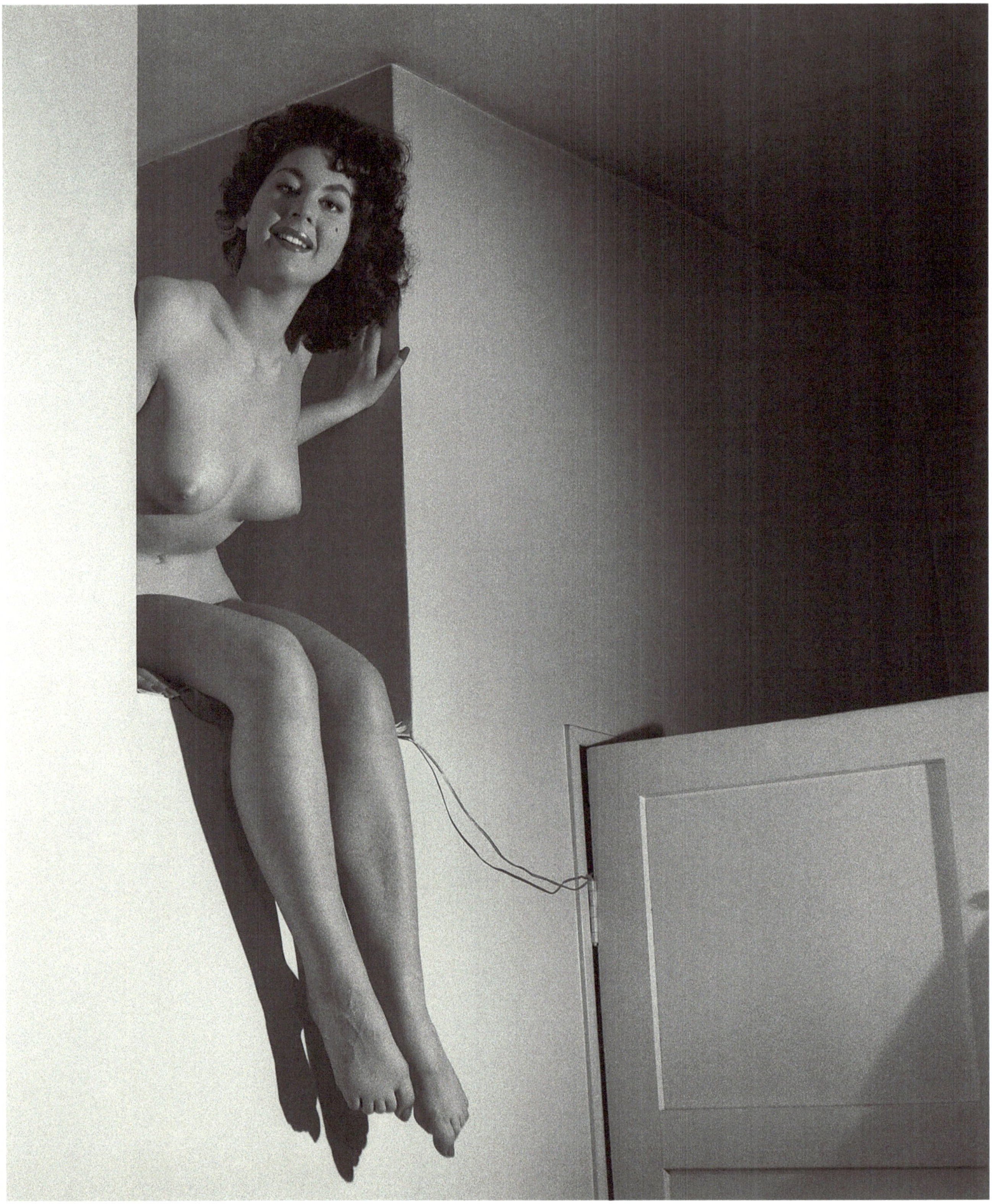

Above and right: Lee Sothern.

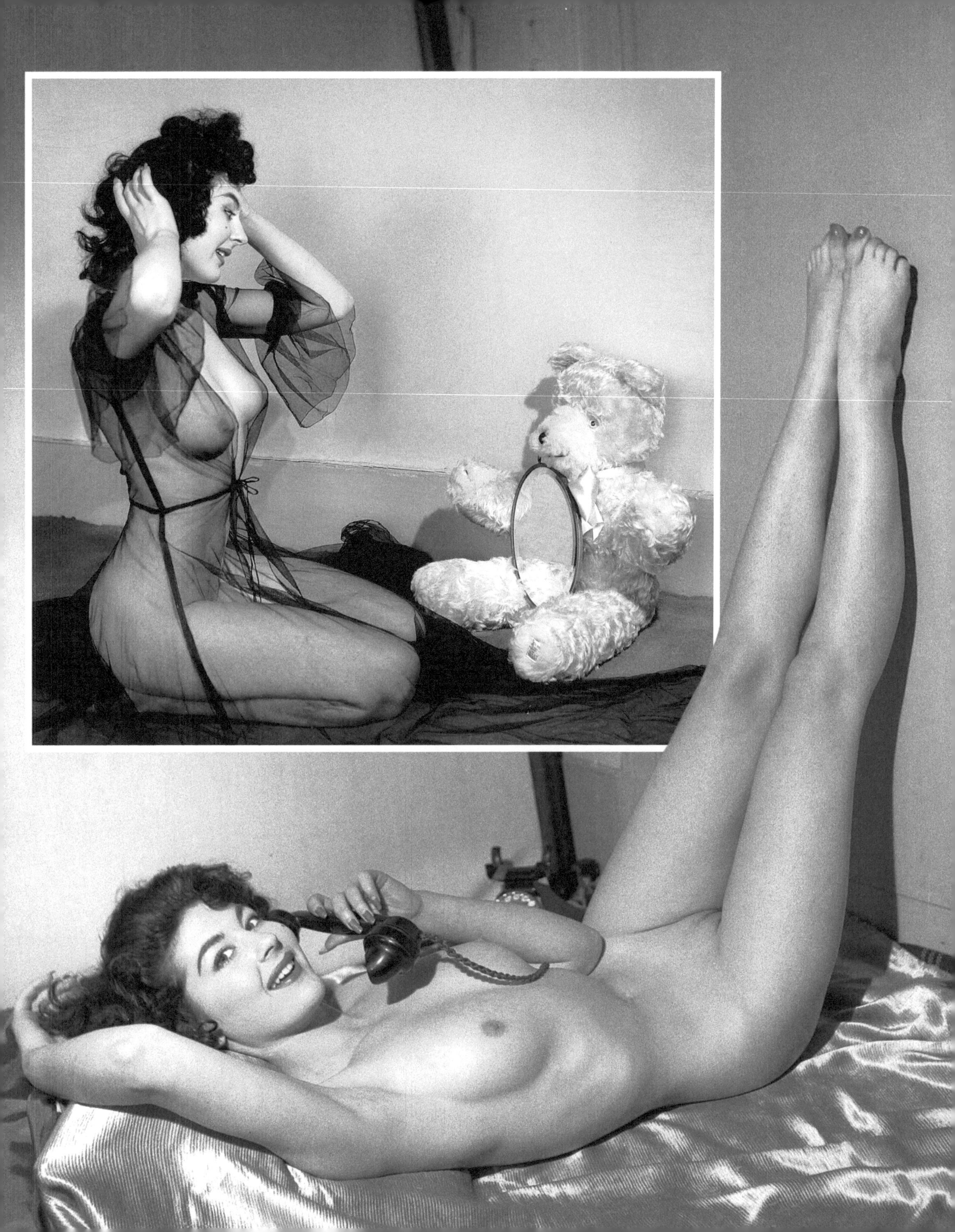

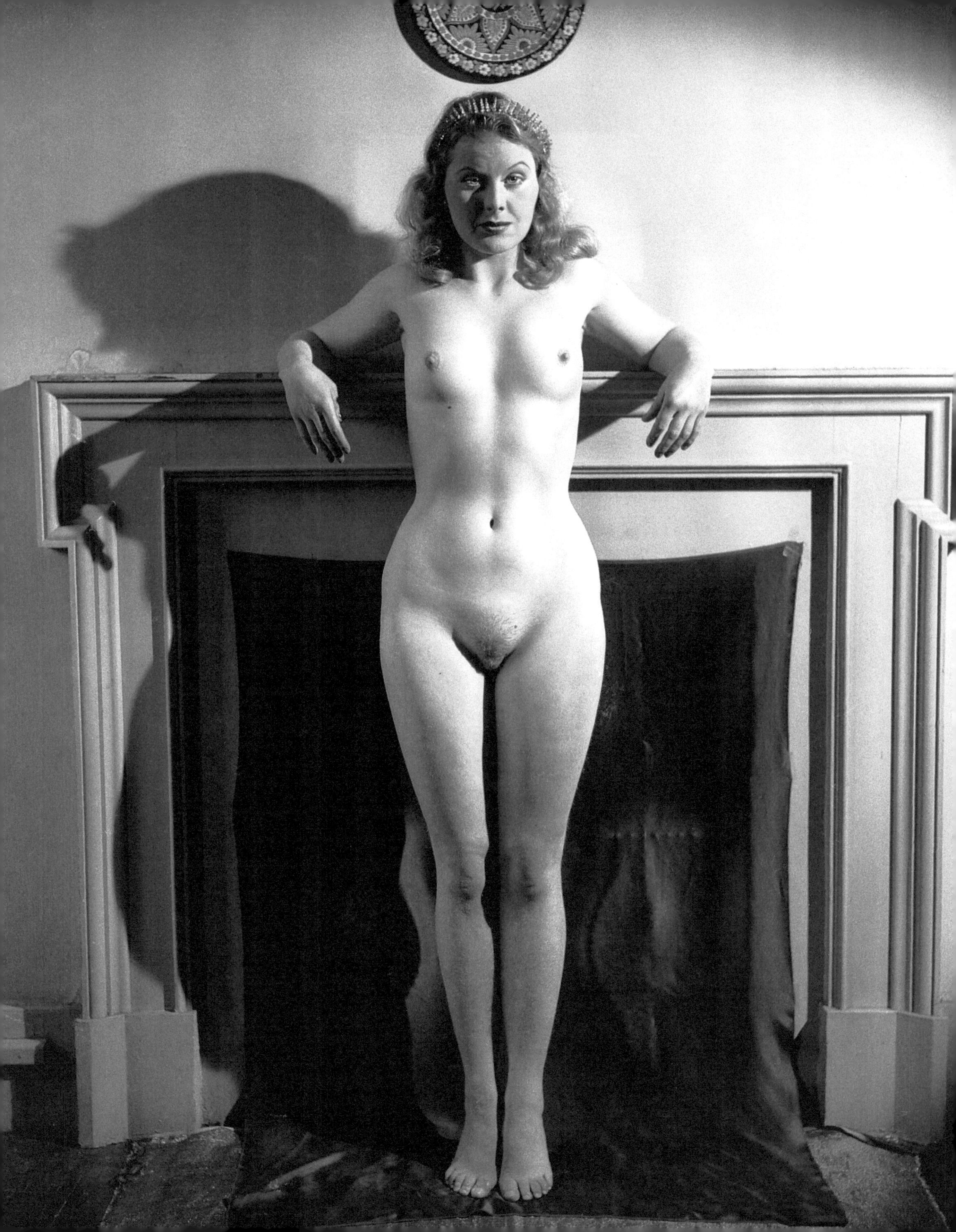

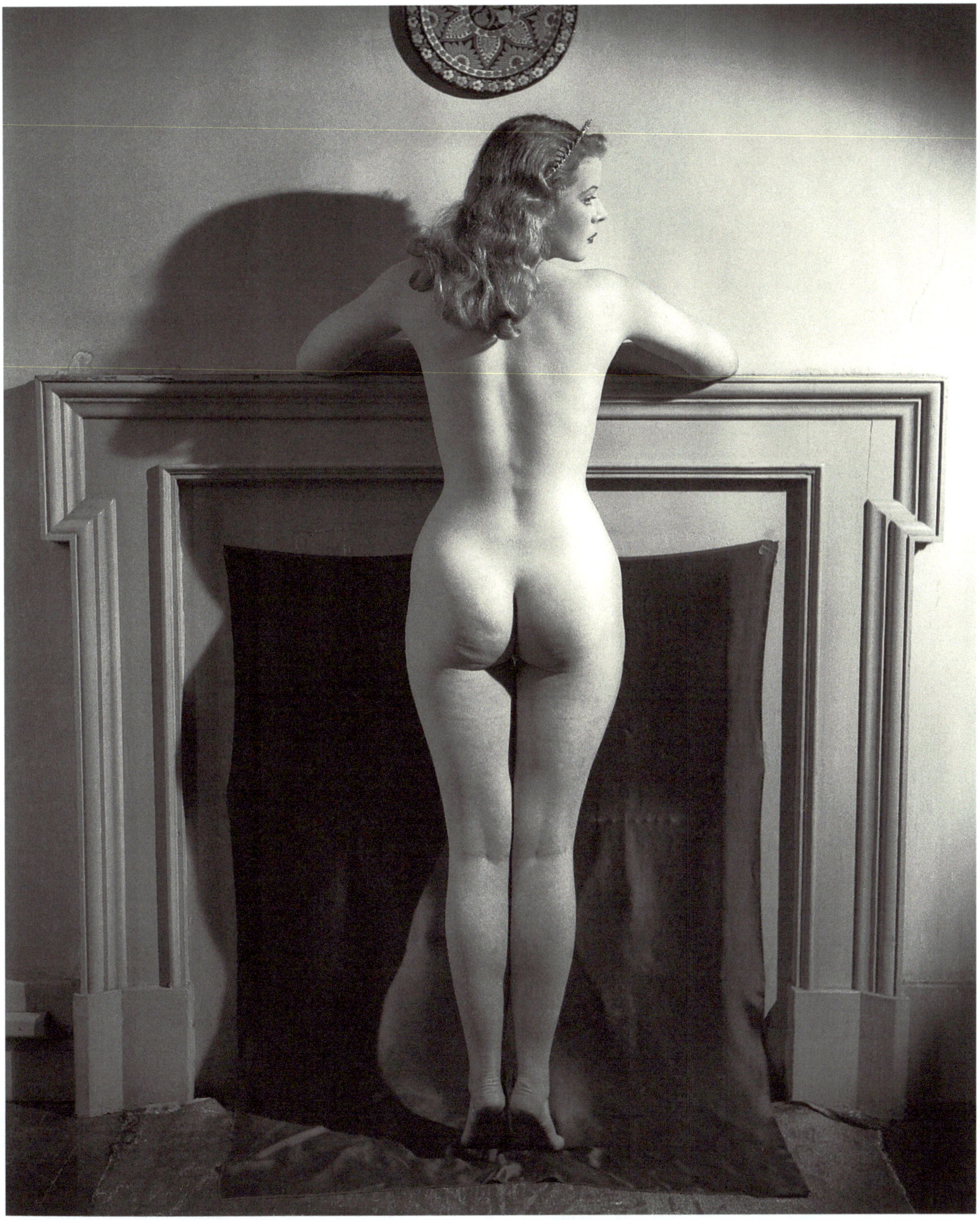

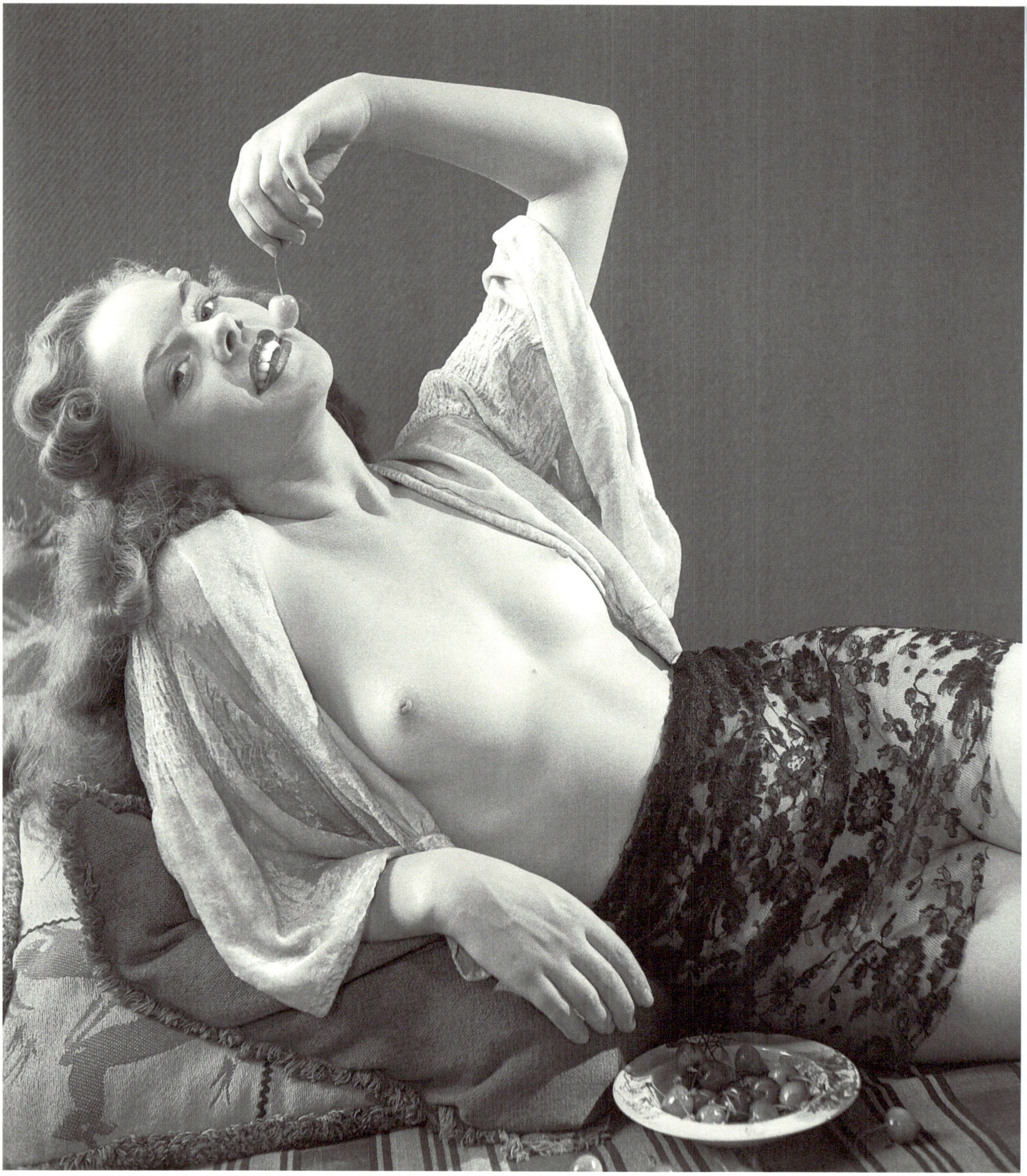

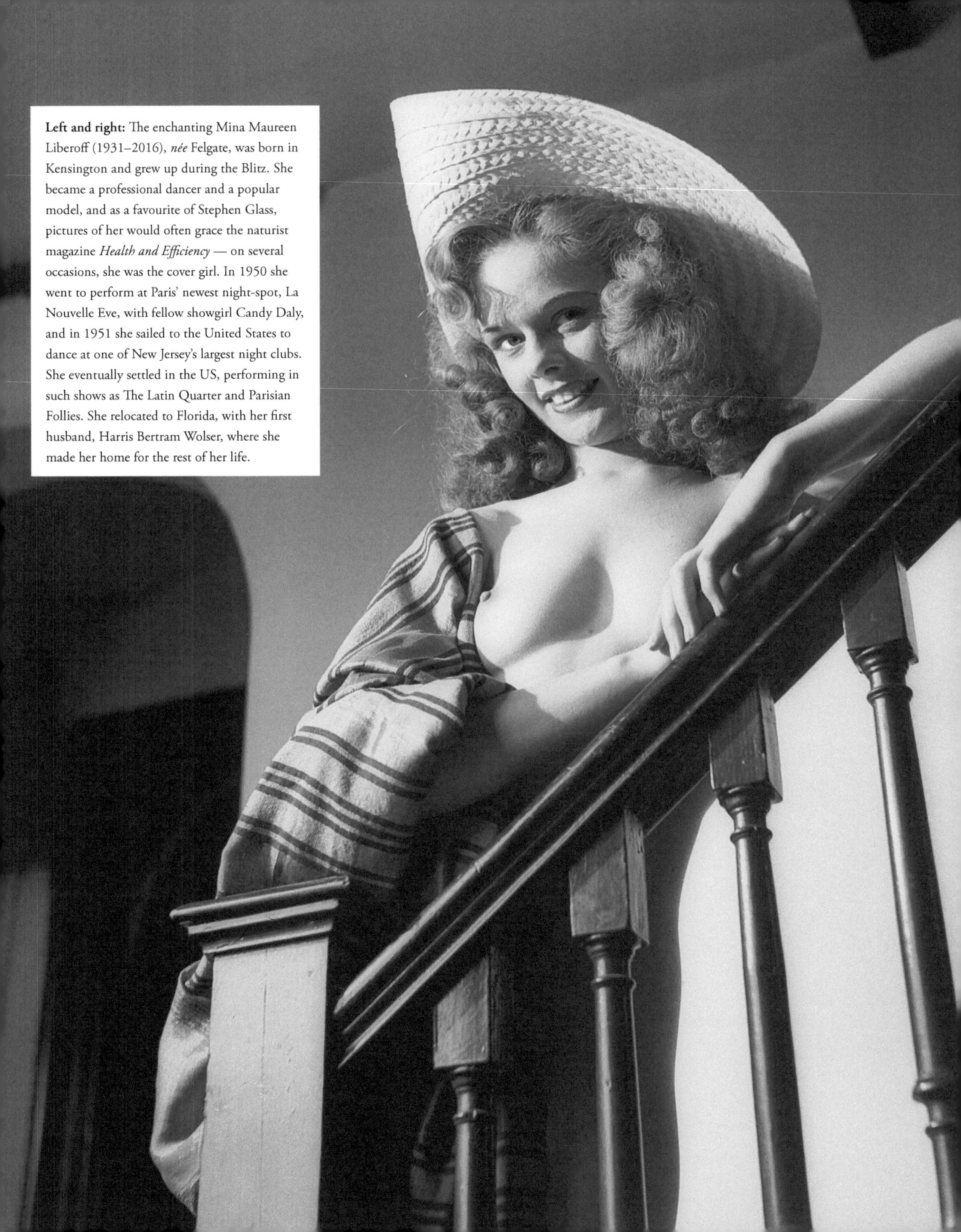

Left and right: The enchanting Mina Maureen Liberoff (1931–2016), *née* Felgate, was born in Kensington and grew up during the Blitz. She became a professional dancer and a popular model, and as a favourite of Stephen Glass, pictures of her would often grace the naturist magazine *Health and Efficiency* — on several occasions, she was the cover girl. In 1950 she went to perform at Paris' newest night-spot, La Nouvelle Eve, with fellow showgirl Candy Daly, and in 1951 she sailed to the United States to dance at one of New Jersey's largest night clubs. She eventually settled in the US, performing in such shows as The Latin Quarter and Parisian Follies. She relocated to Florida, with her first husband, Harris Bertram Wolser, where she made her home for the rest of her life.

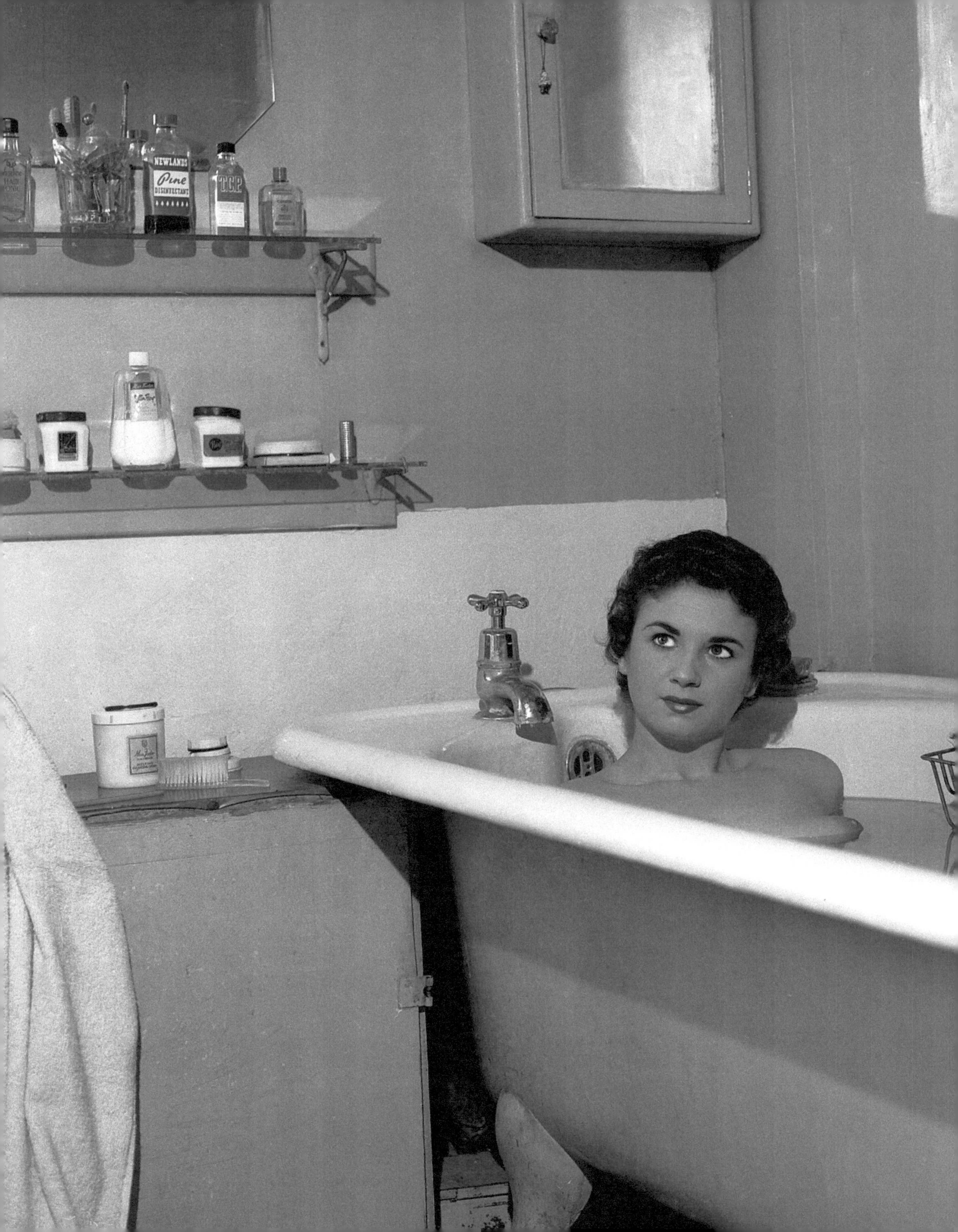
NEWLANDS
Pine
DISINFECTANT
T.C.P.

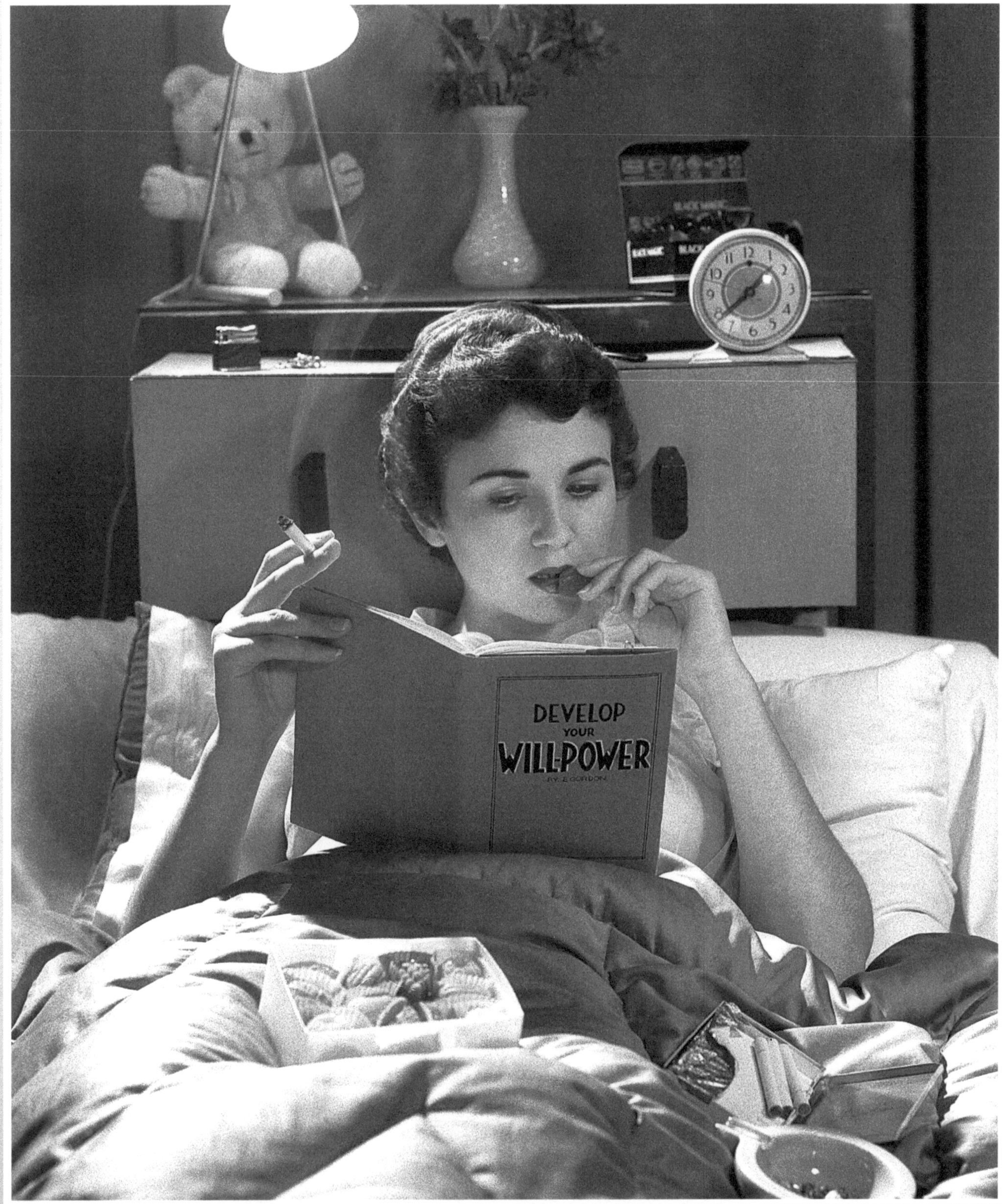

Left and above: Splish splash and time for bed — Anita Smith.

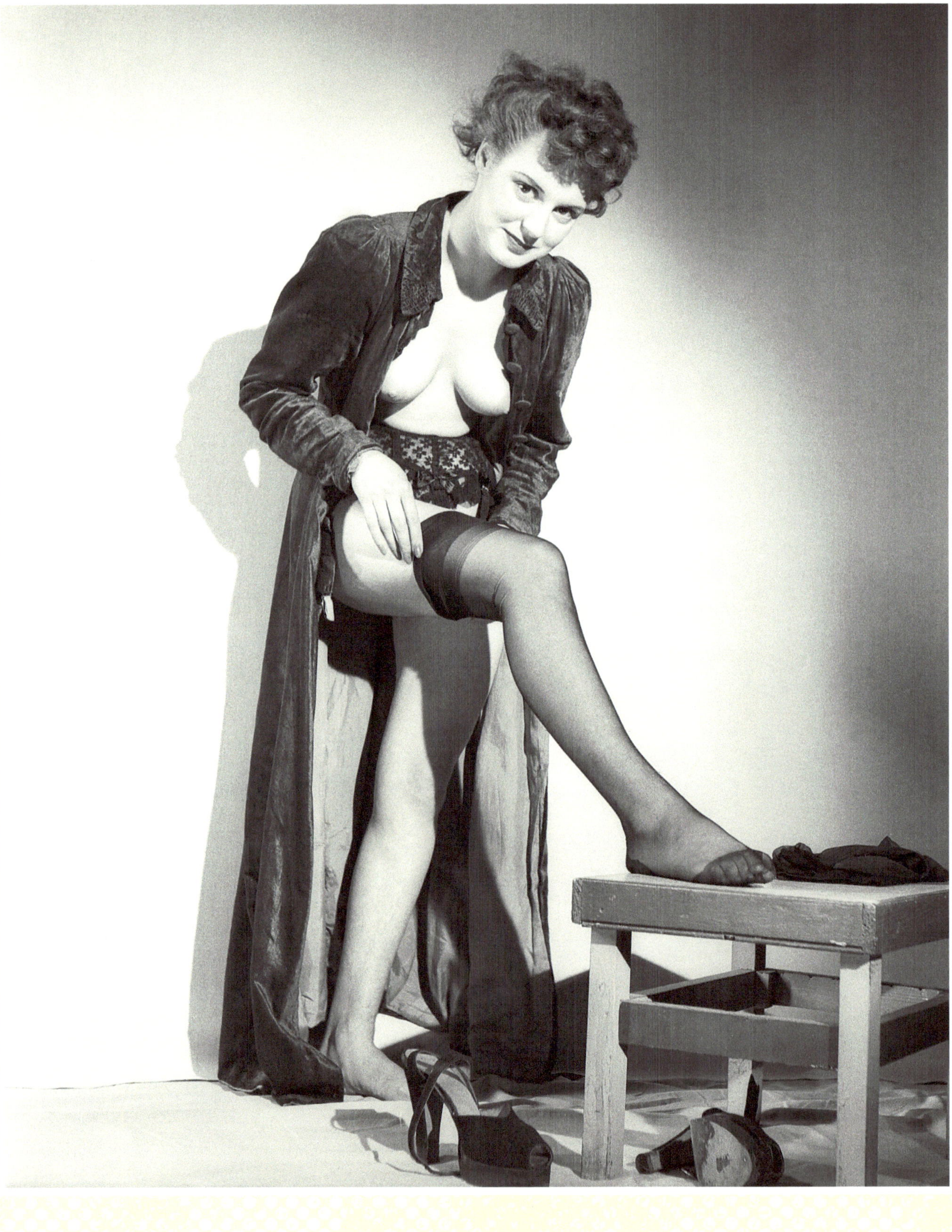

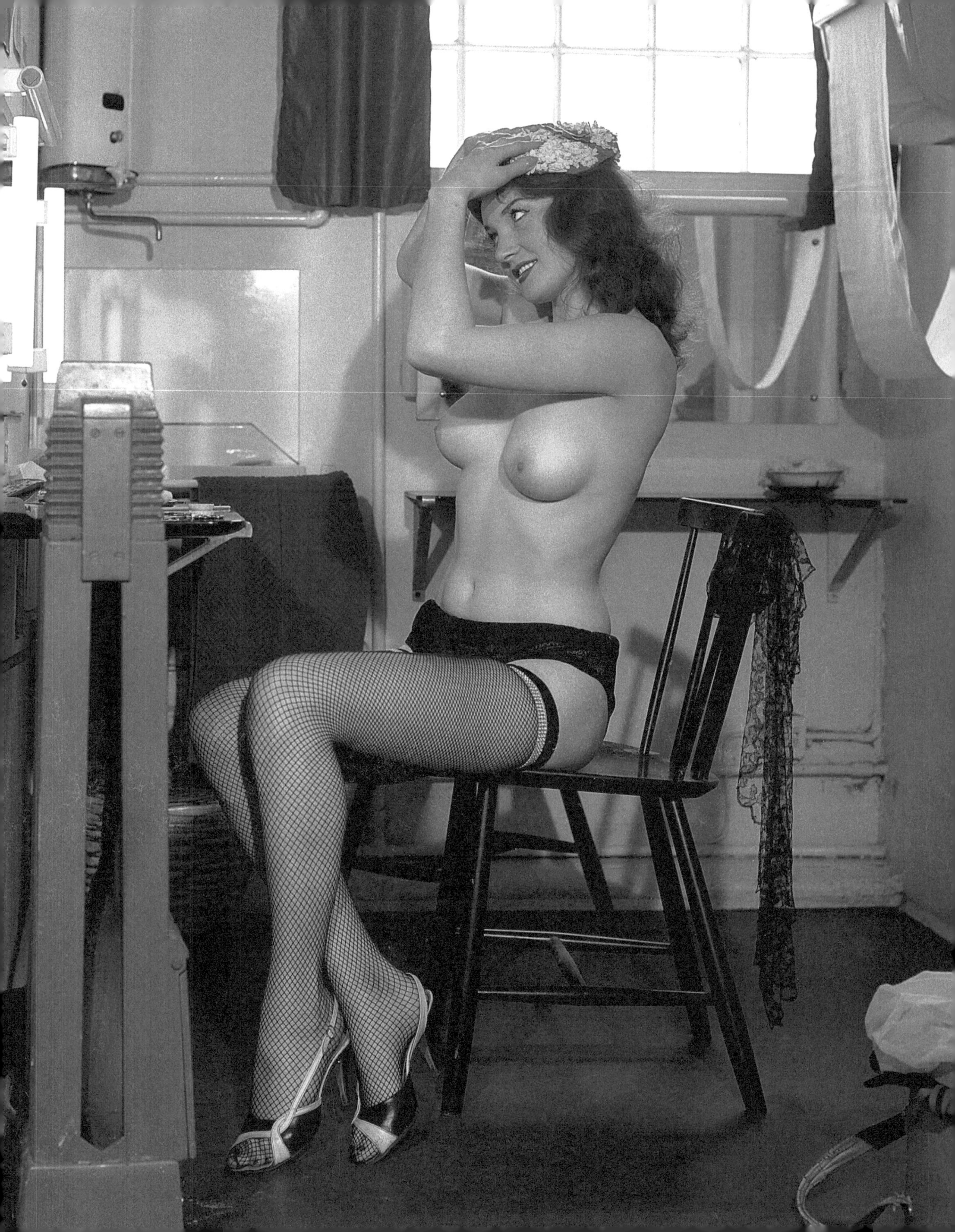

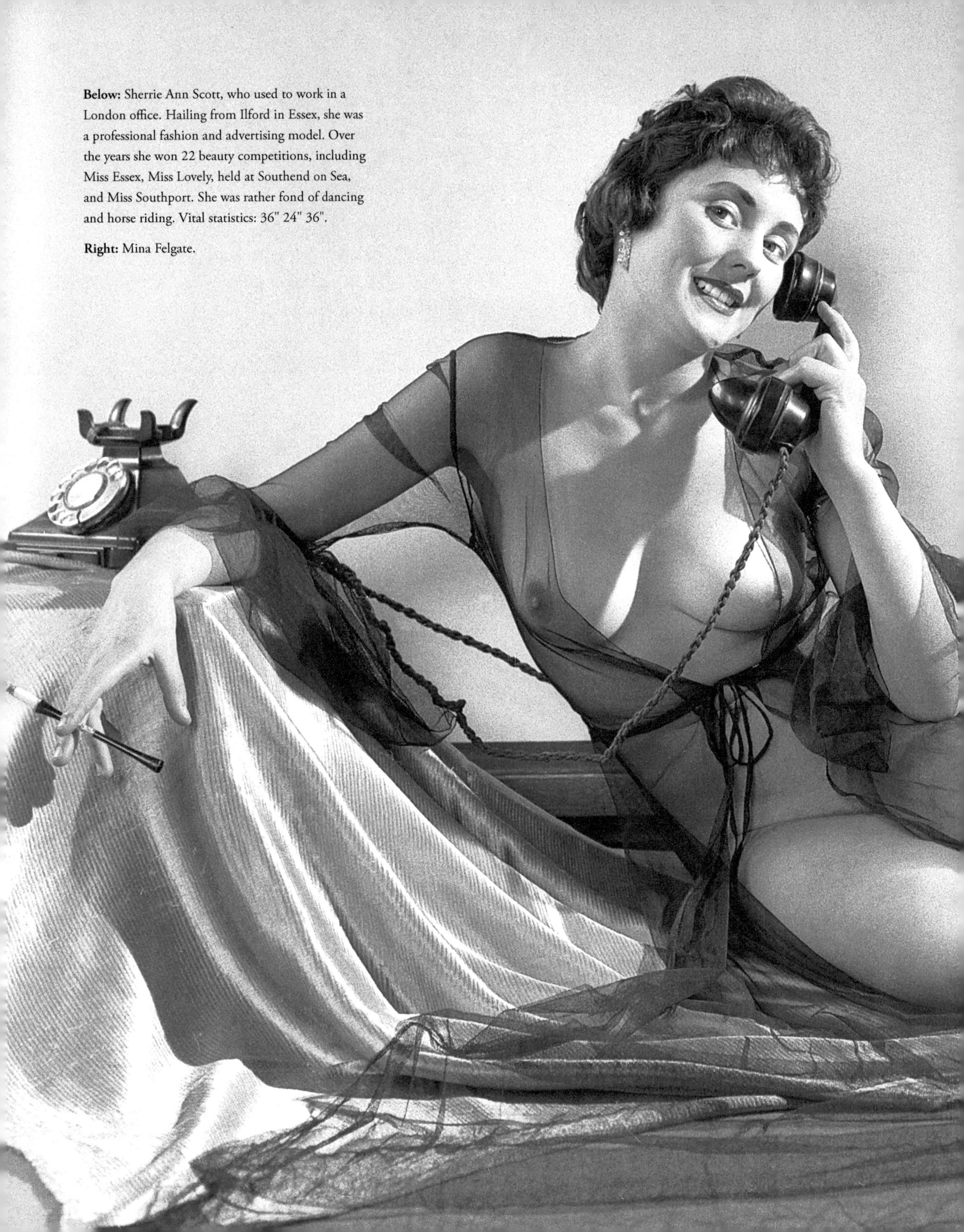

Below: Sherrie Ann Scott, who used to work in a London office. Hailing from Ilford in Essex, she was a professional fashion and advertising model. Over the years she won 22 beauty competitions, including Miss Essex, Miss Lovely, held at Southend on Sea, and Miss Southport. She was rather fond of dancing and horse riding. Vital statistics: 36" 24" 36".

Right: Mina Felgate.

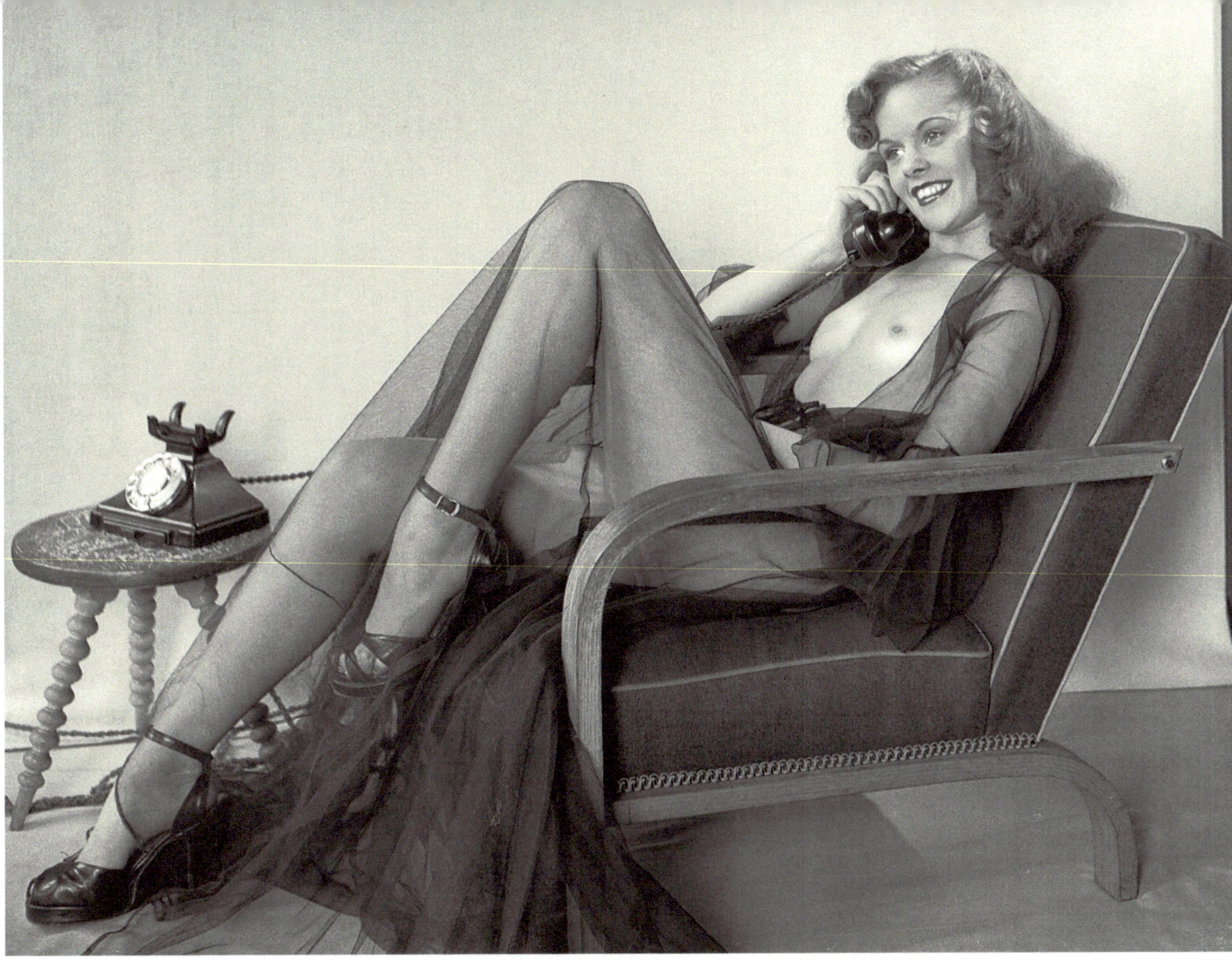

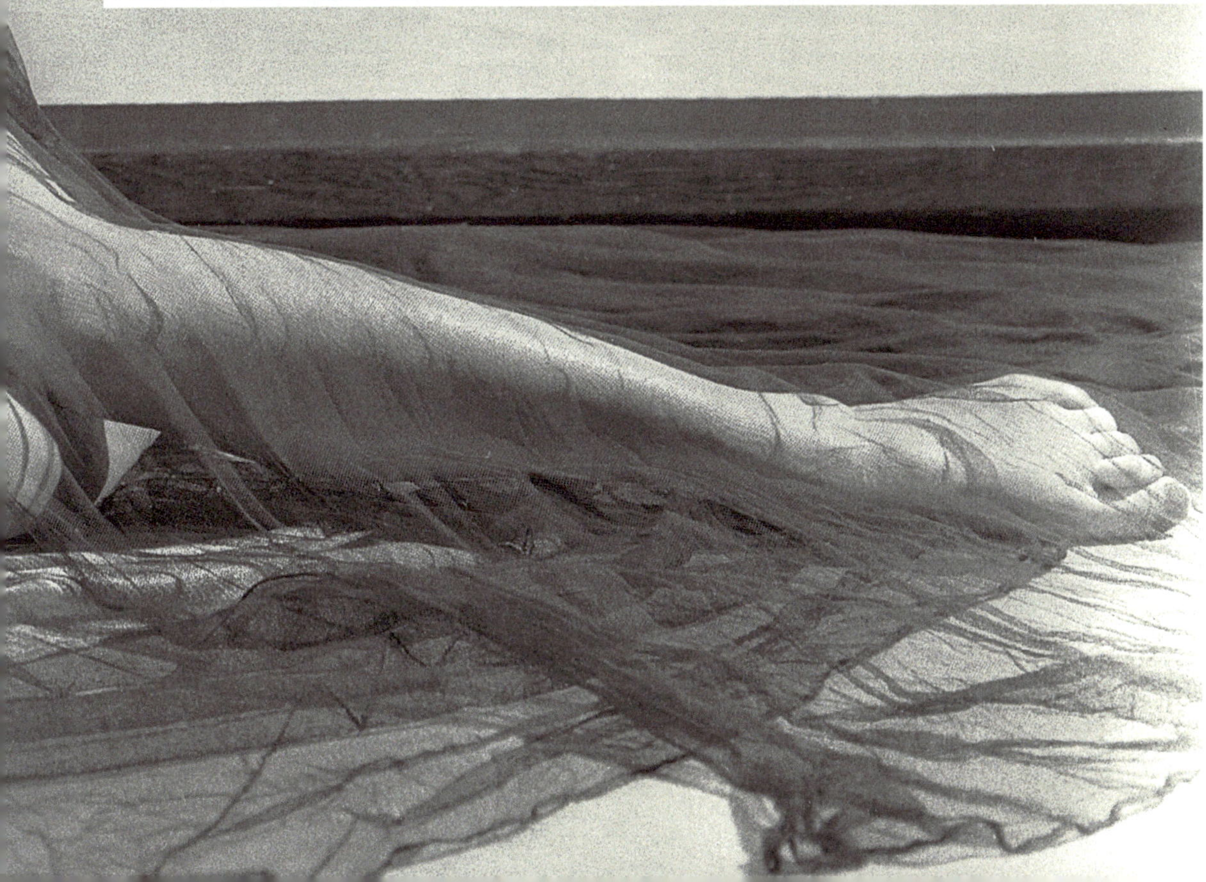

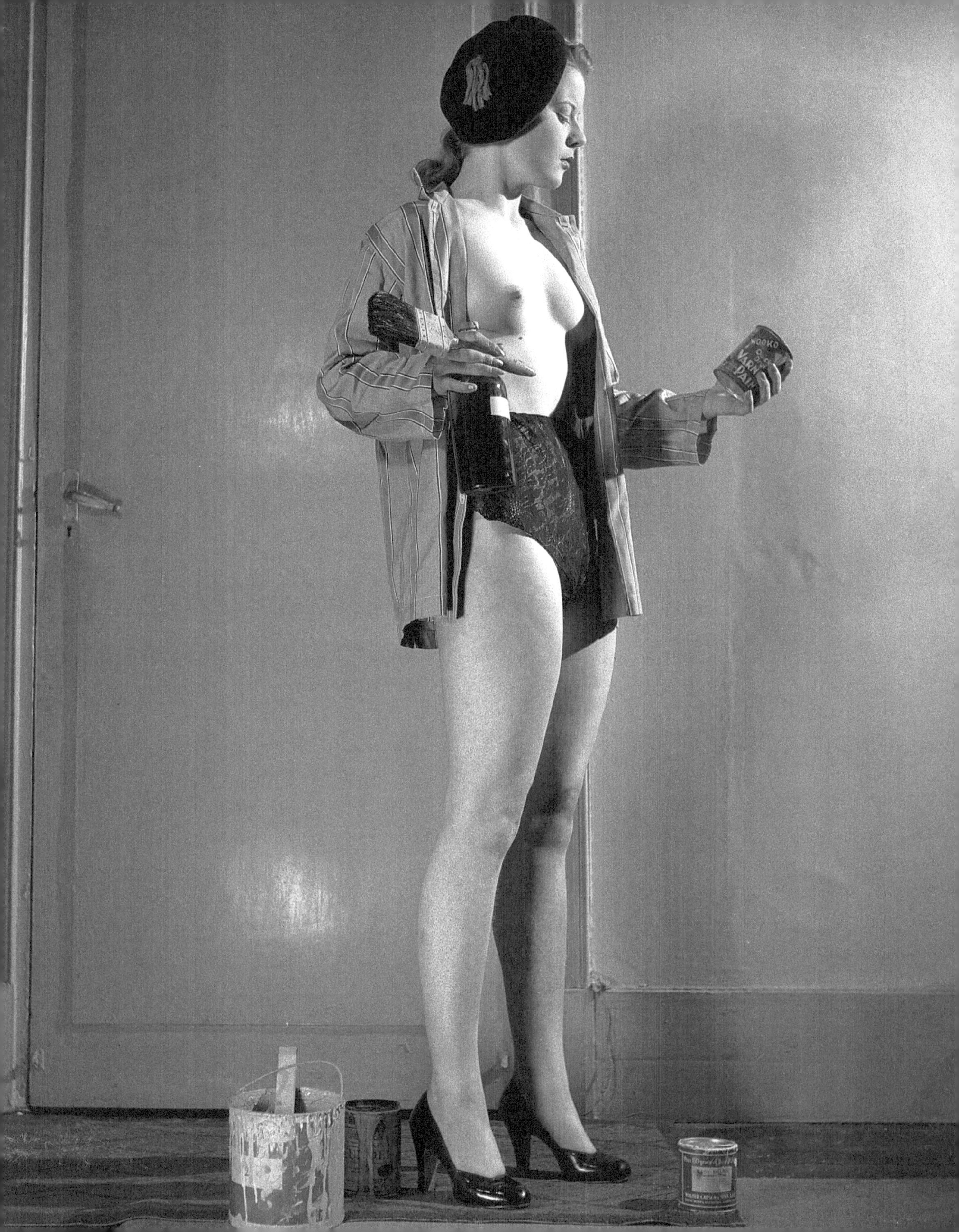

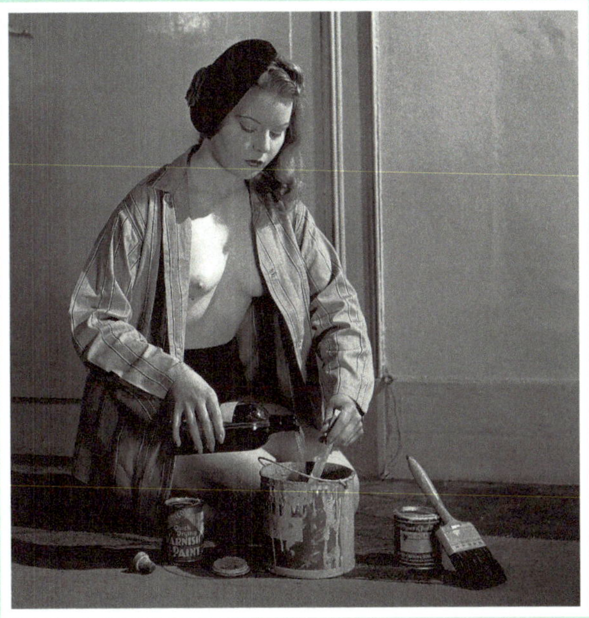

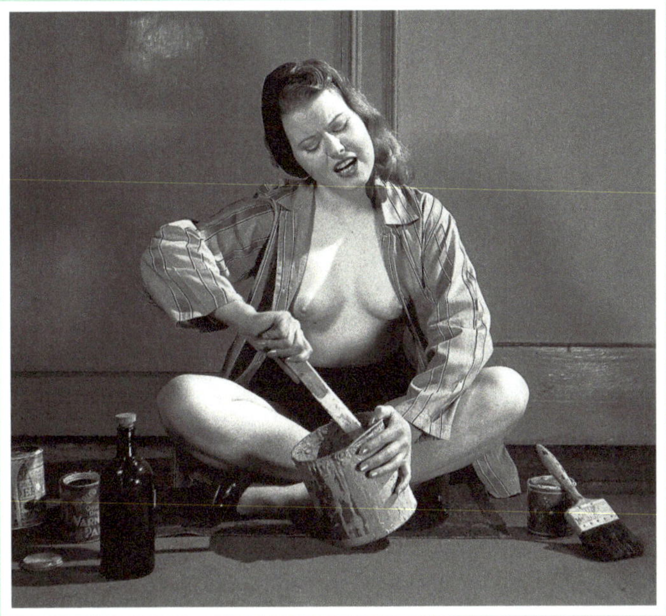

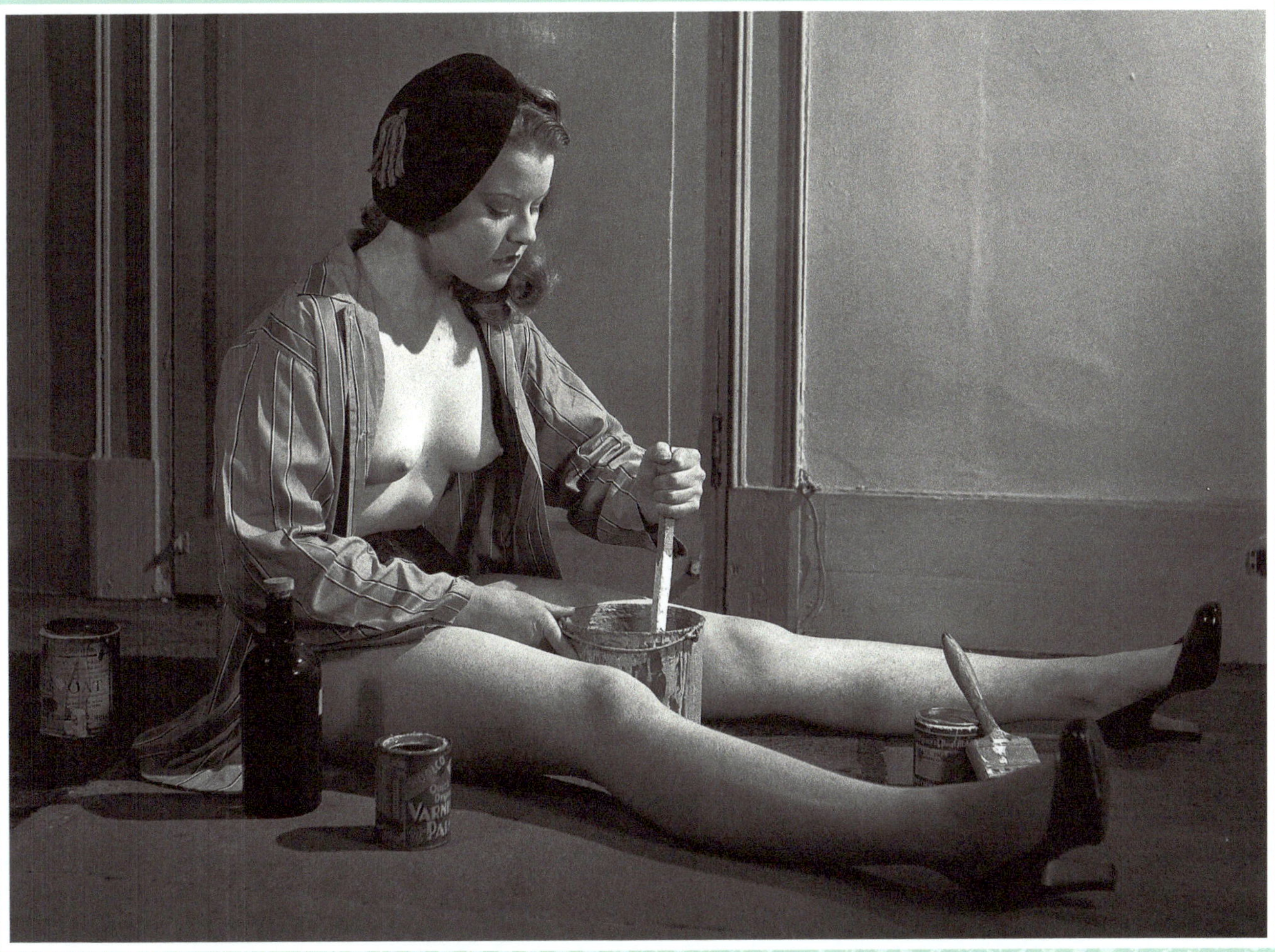

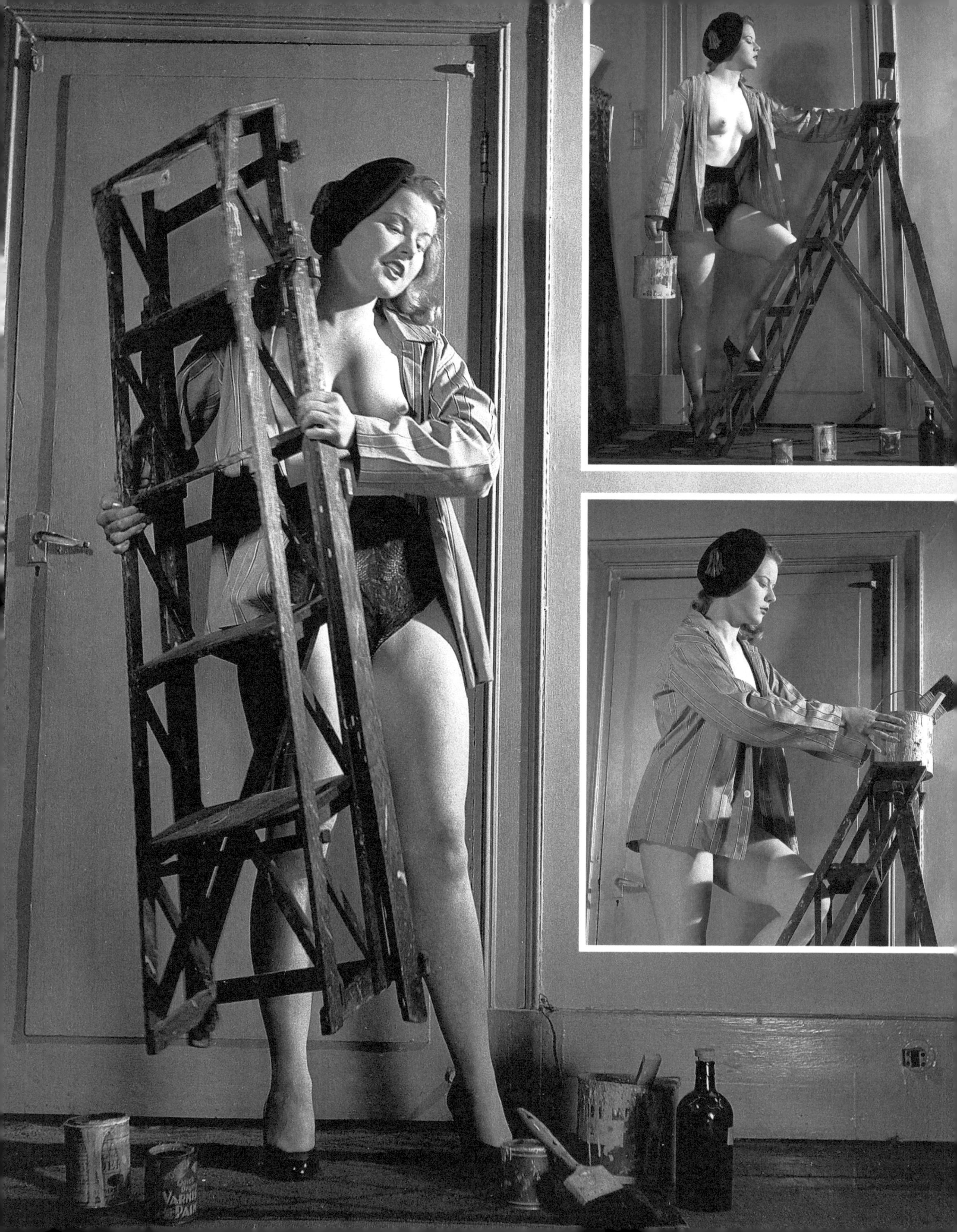

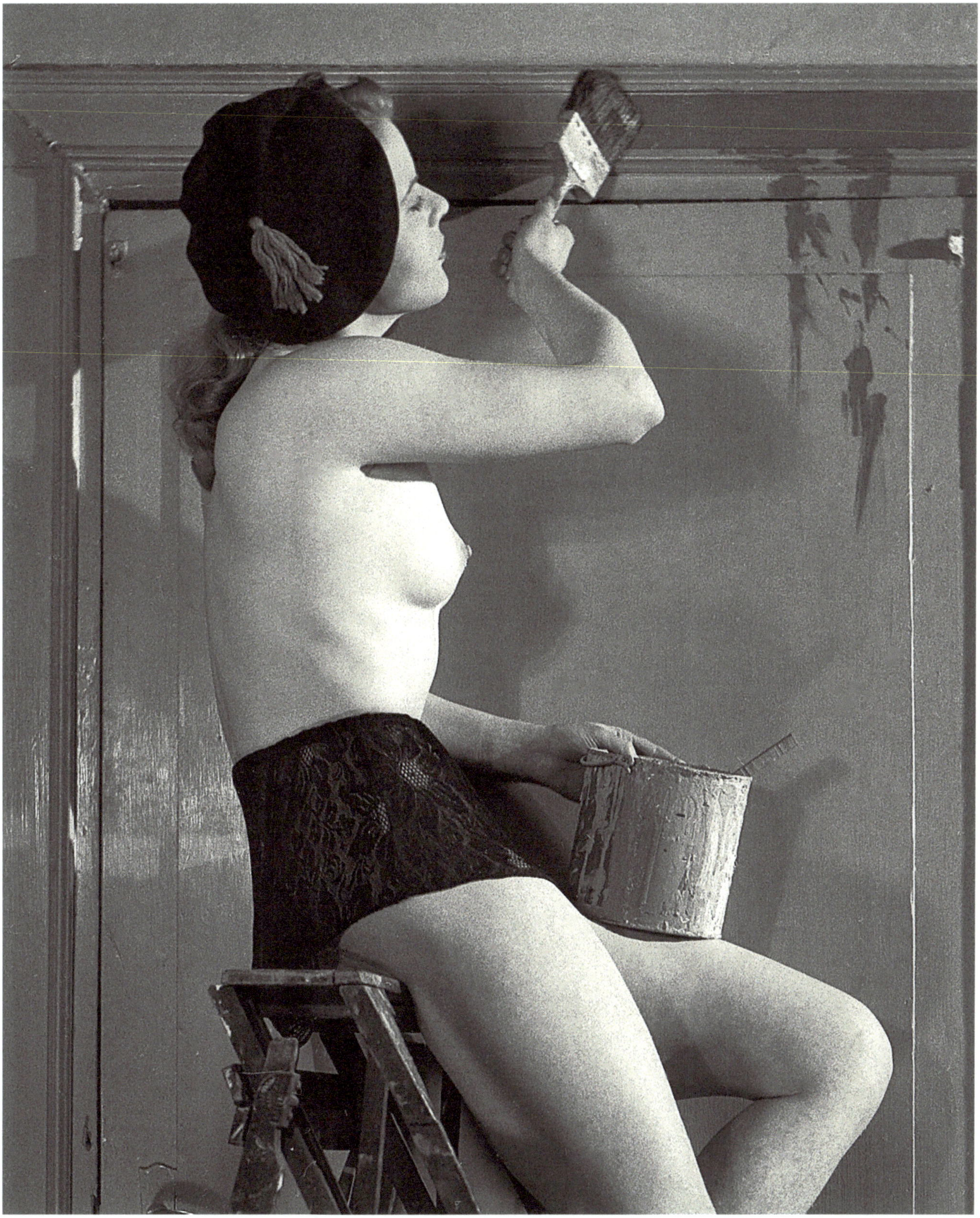

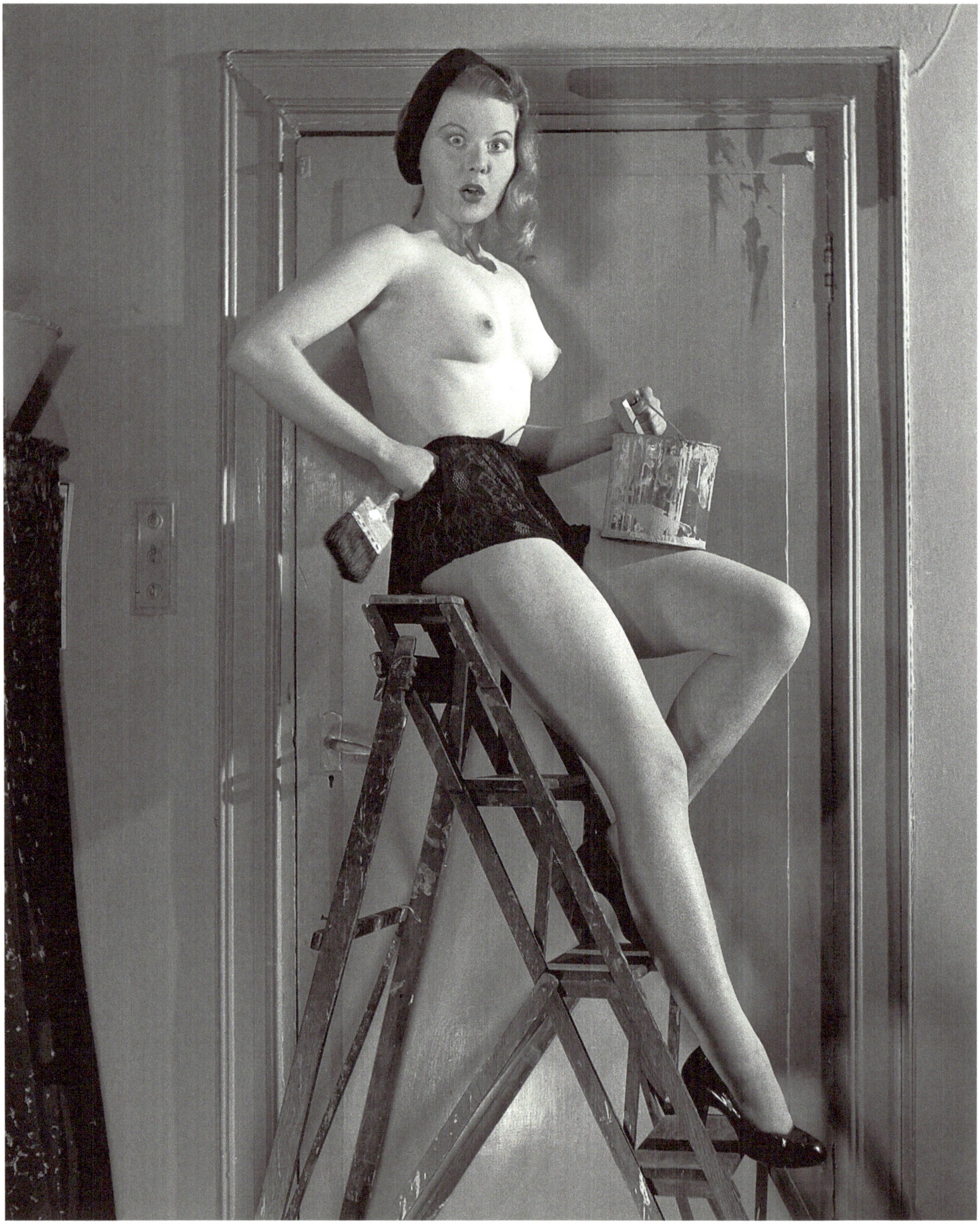

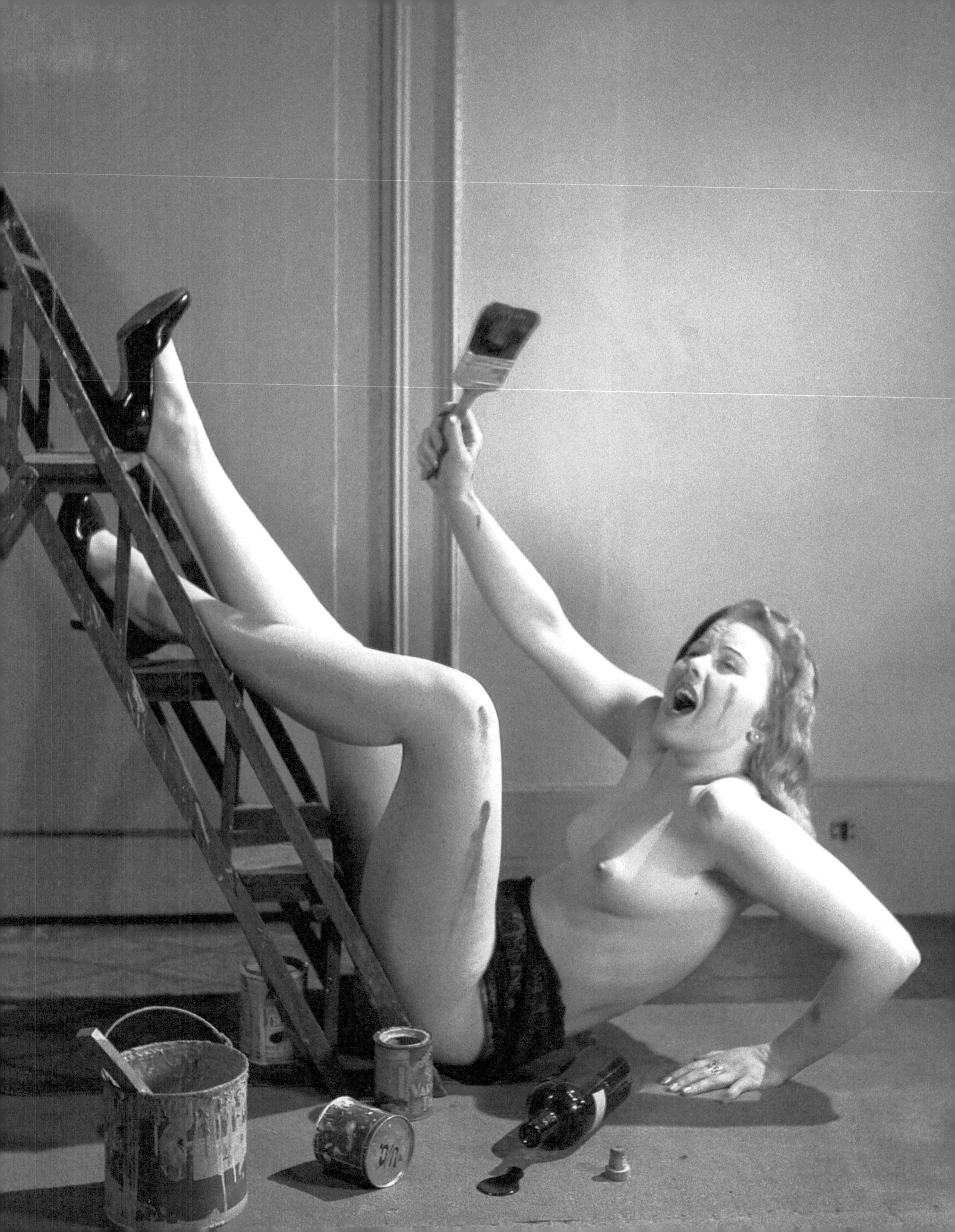

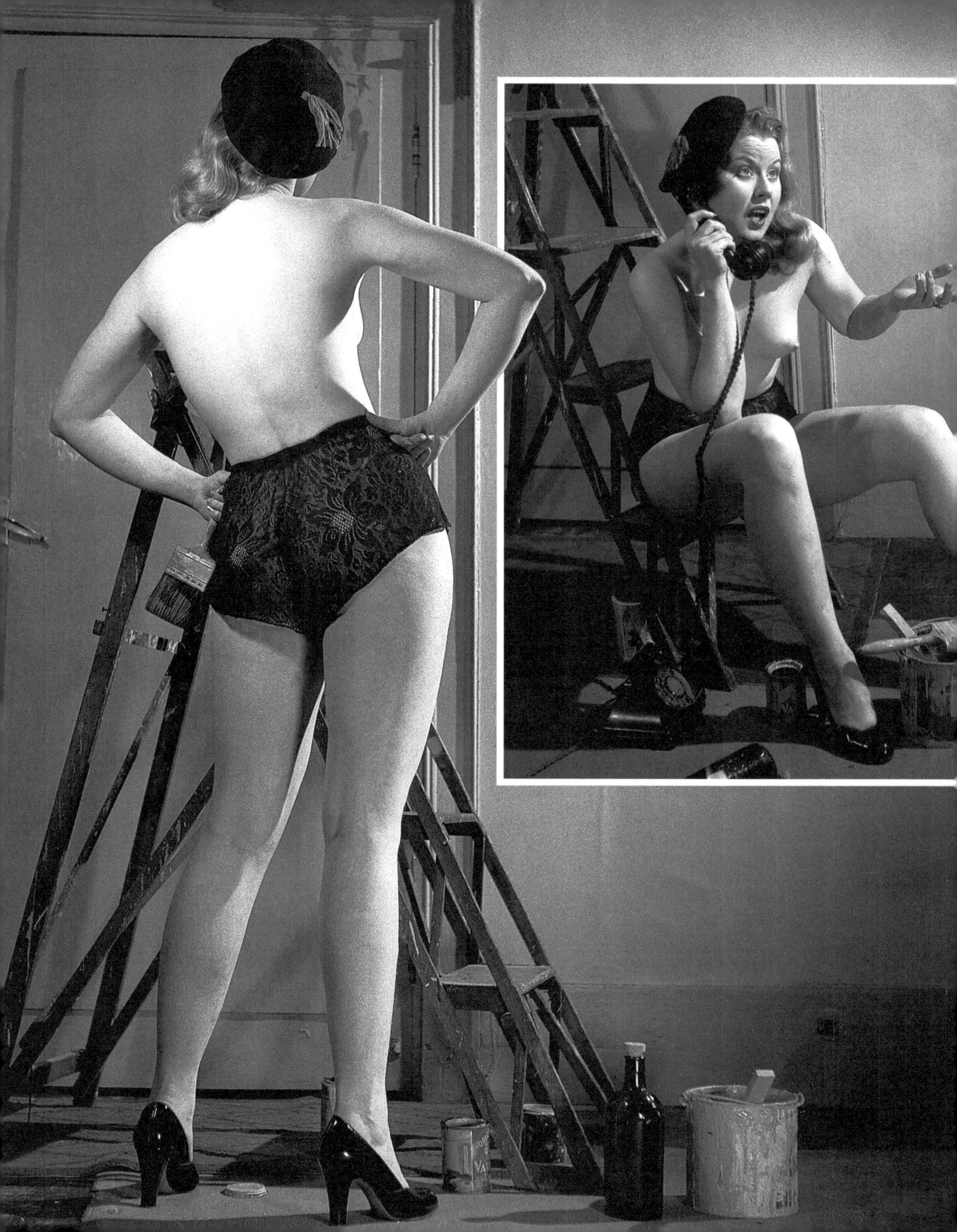

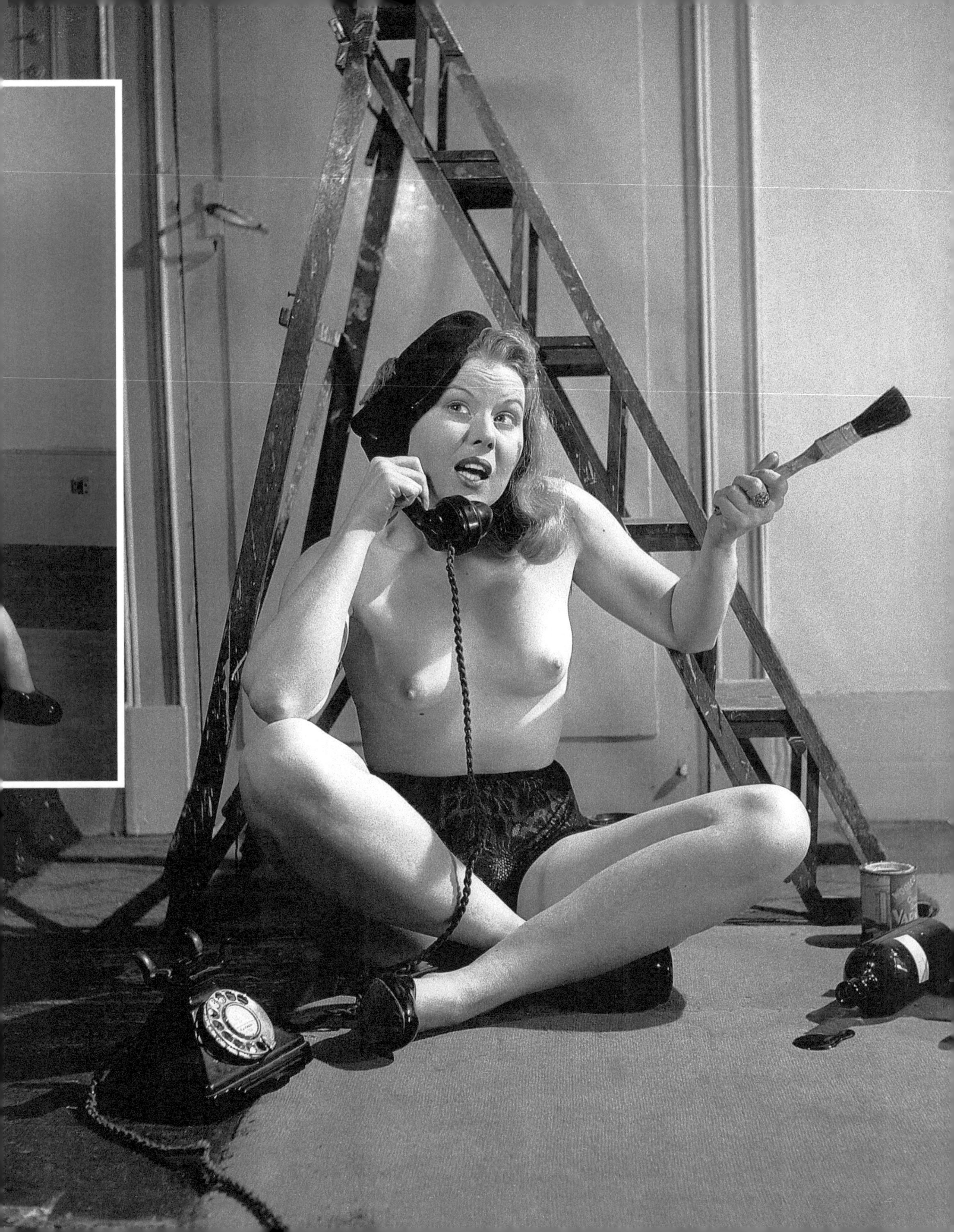

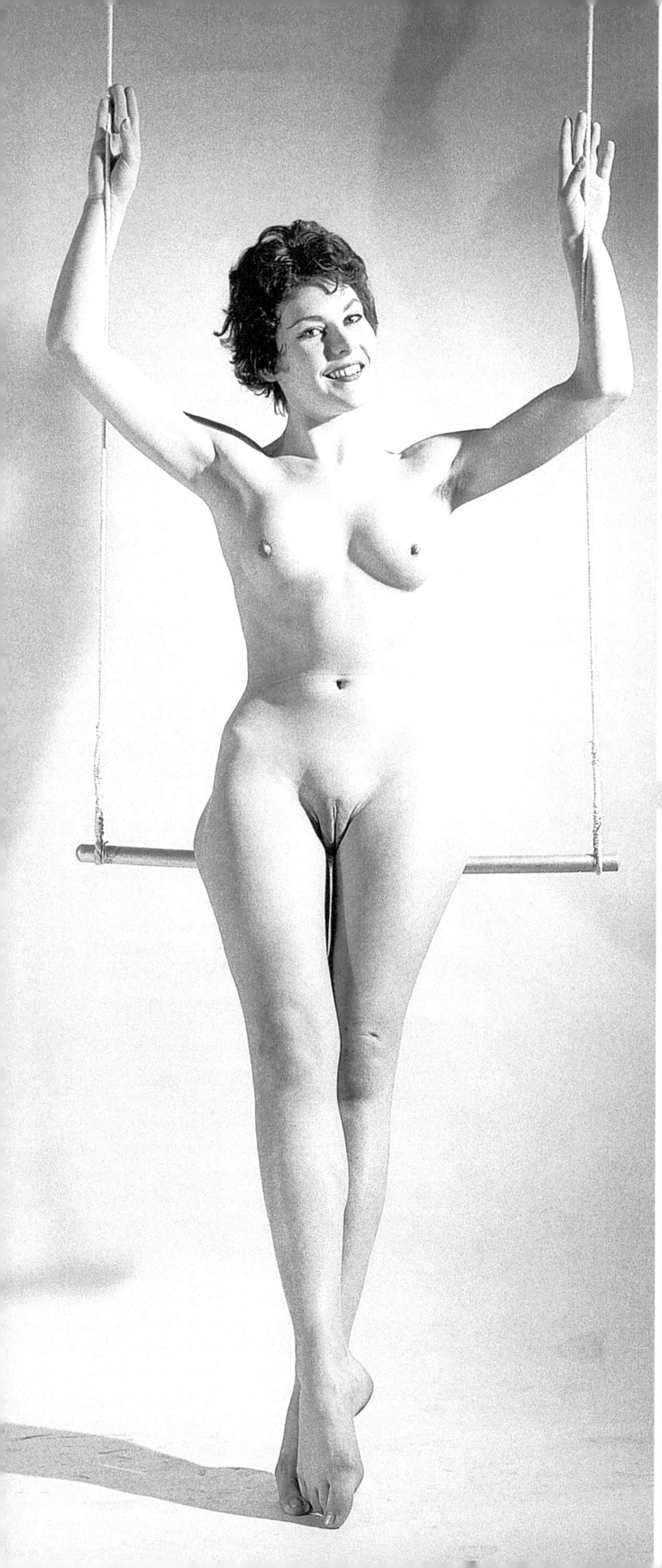
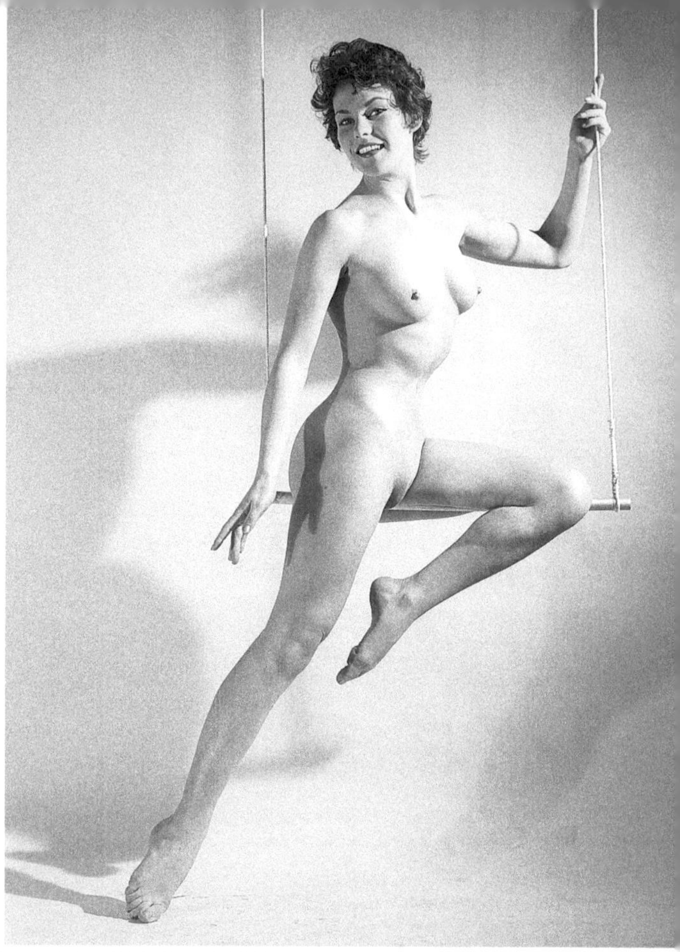
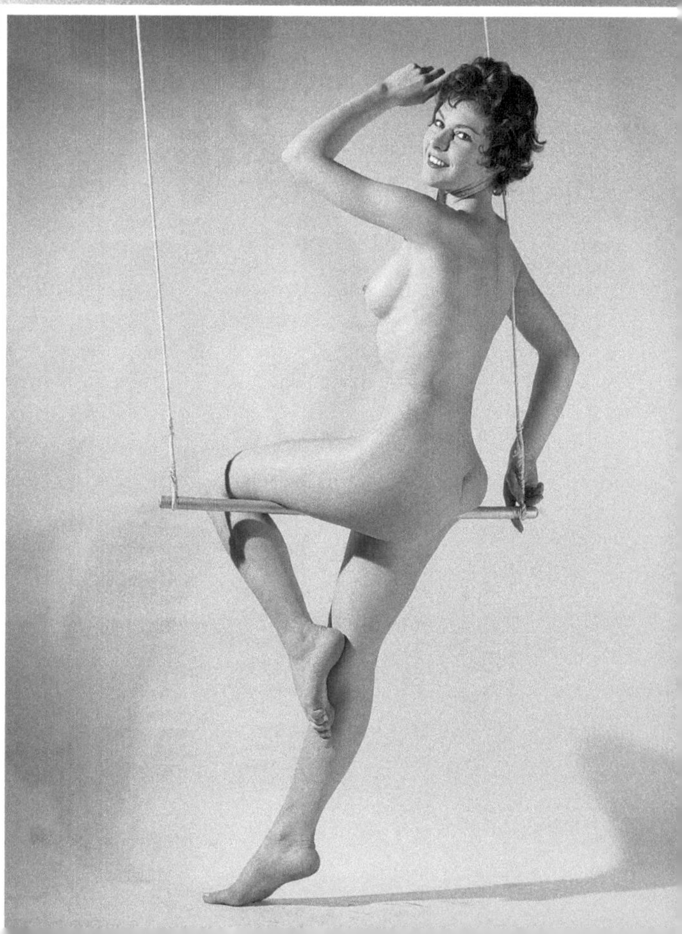

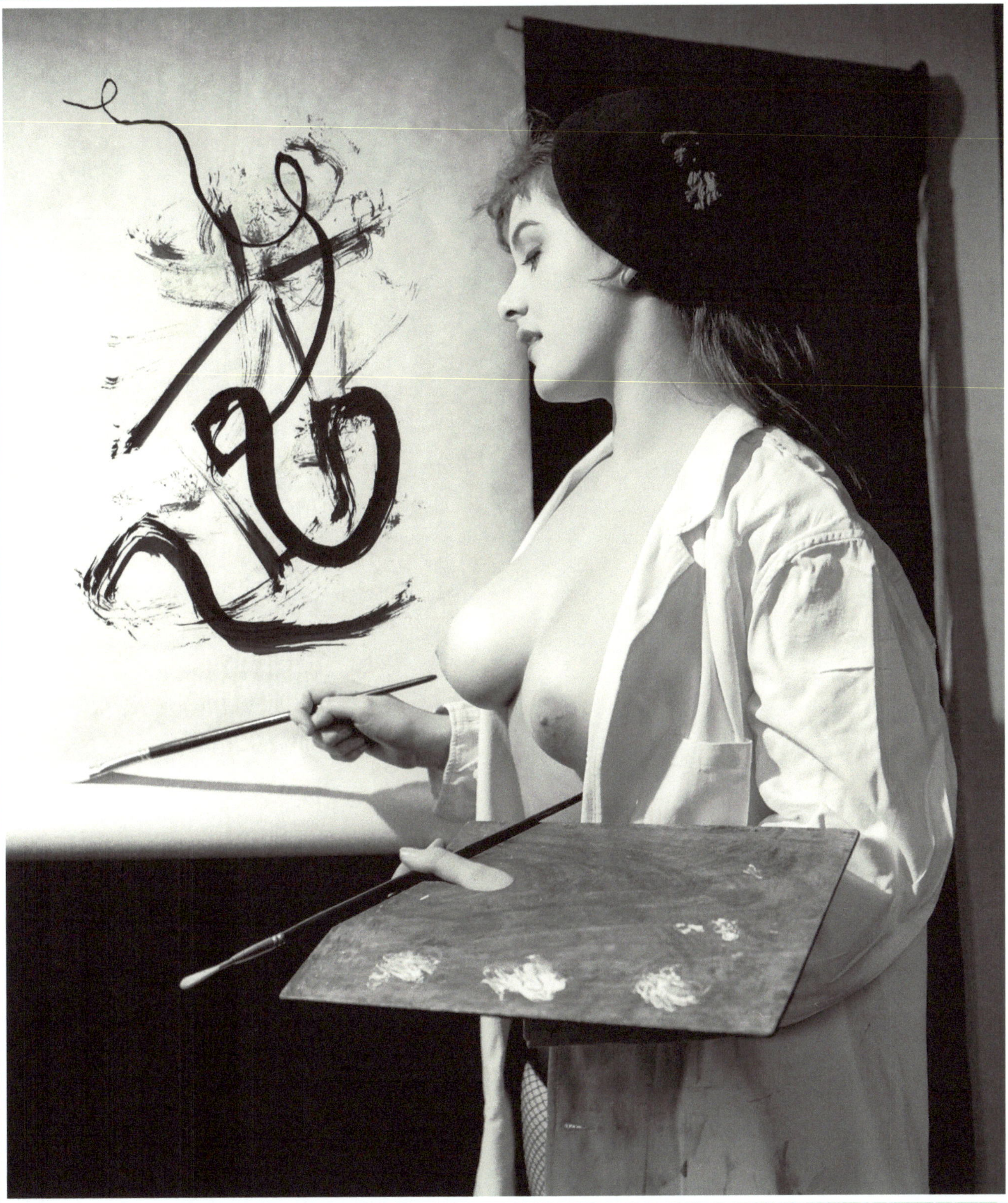

Above: June Wilkinson, notorious London show-girl and model.

Left: June Russell, professional swimmer from Dorset who performed in an Aqua Show on the South Coast, after which she lived in Sutton in Surrey.

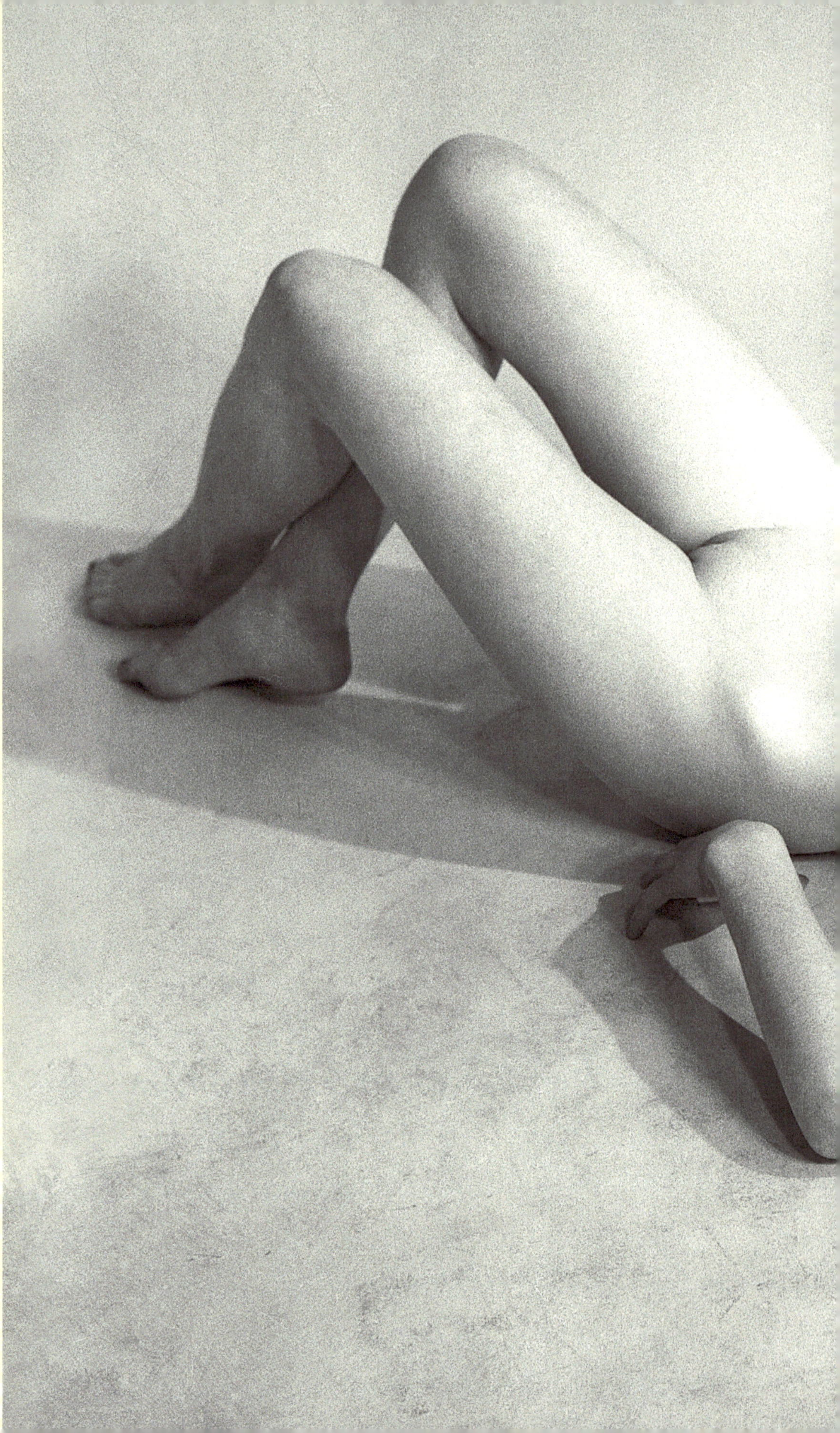

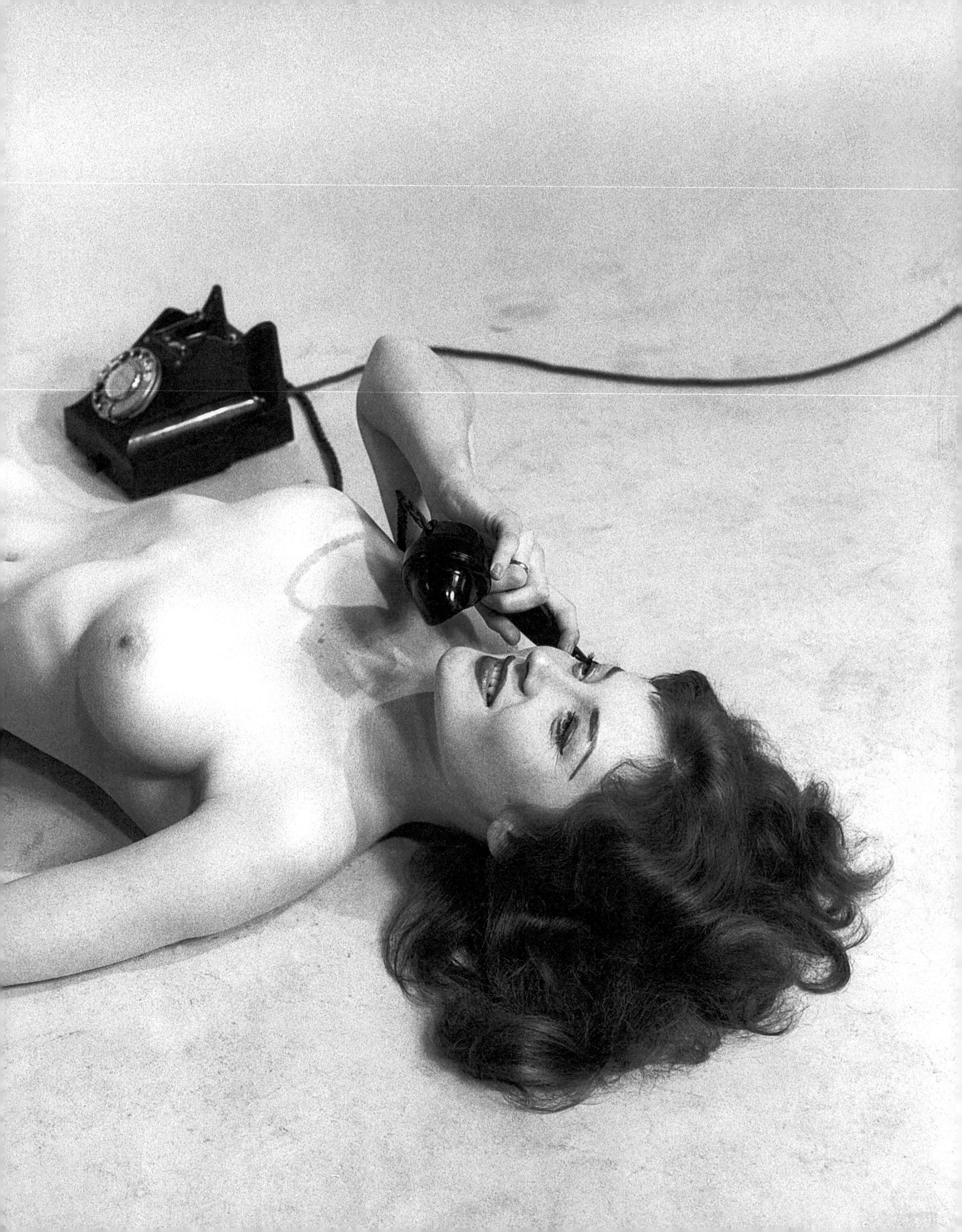

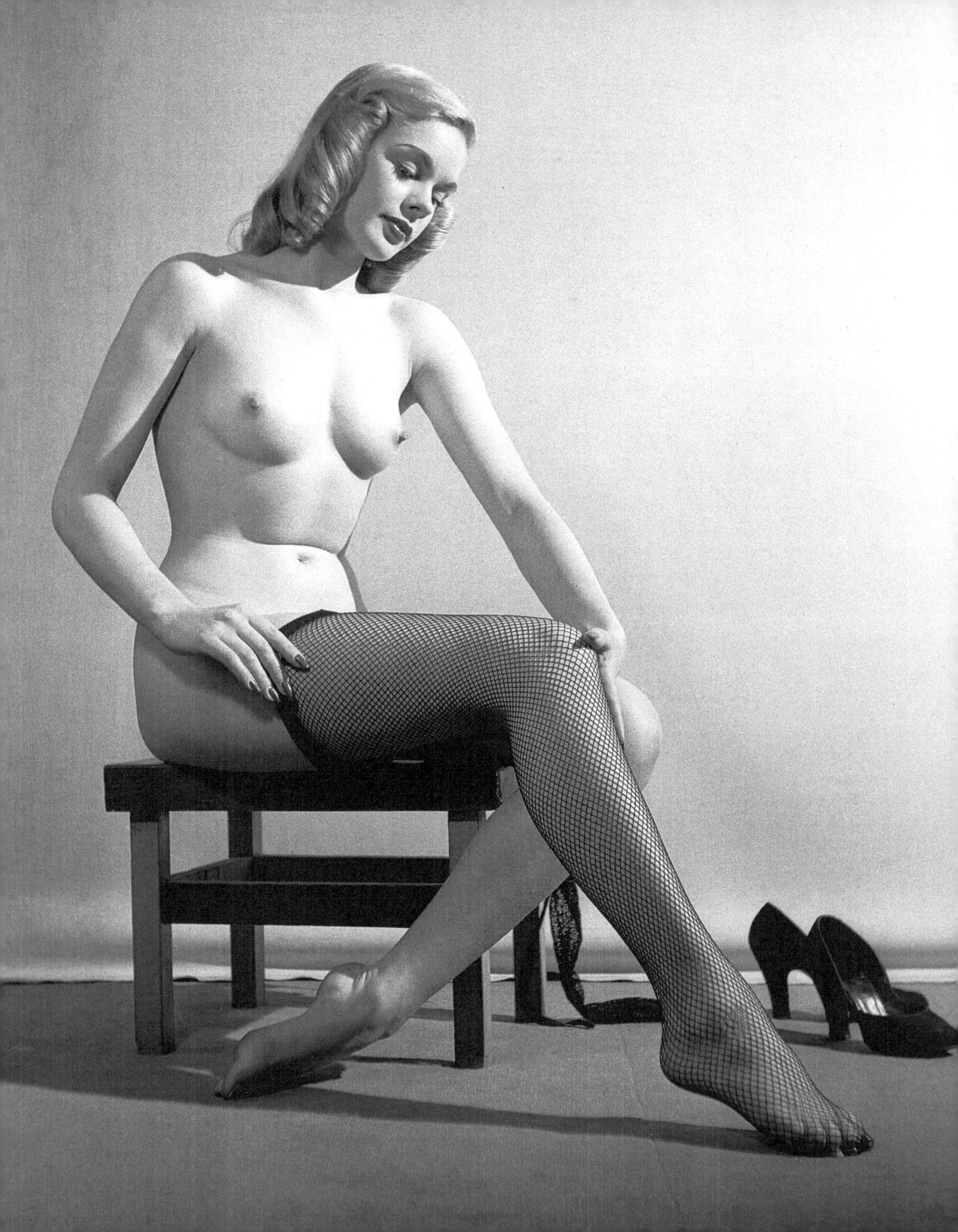

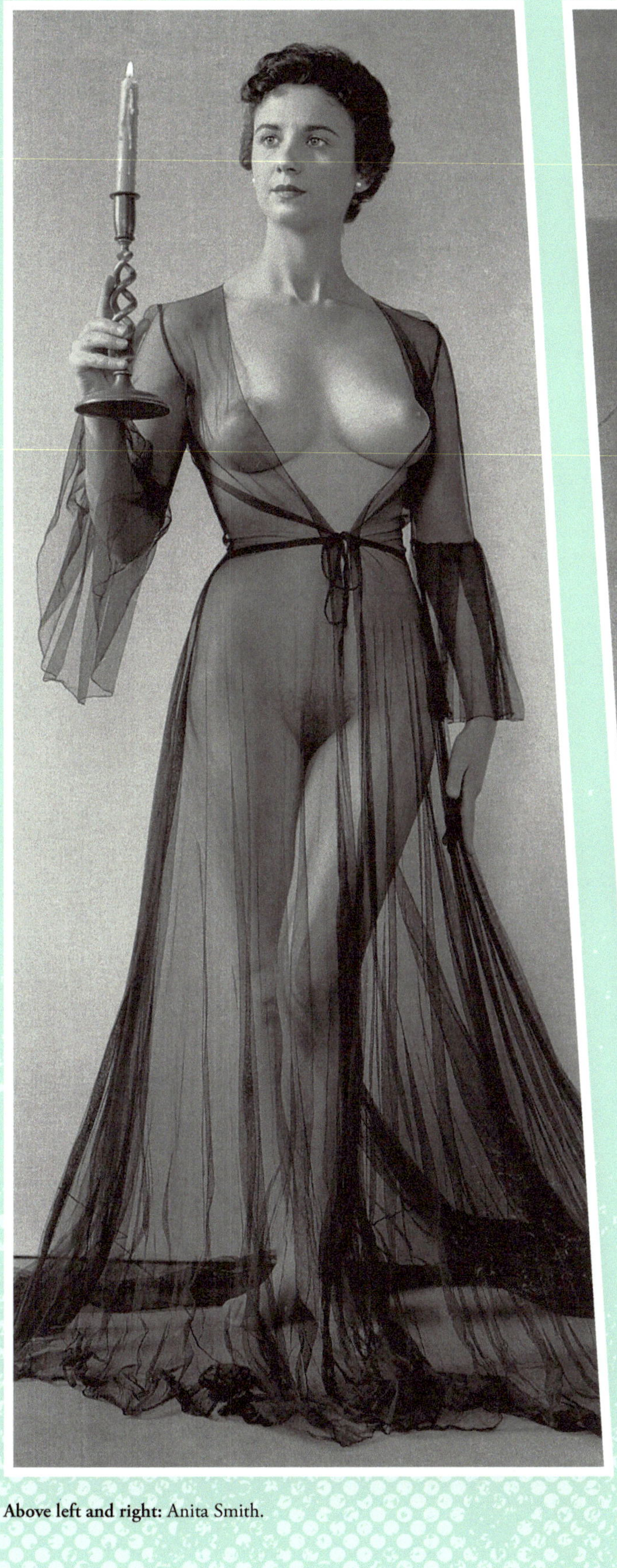

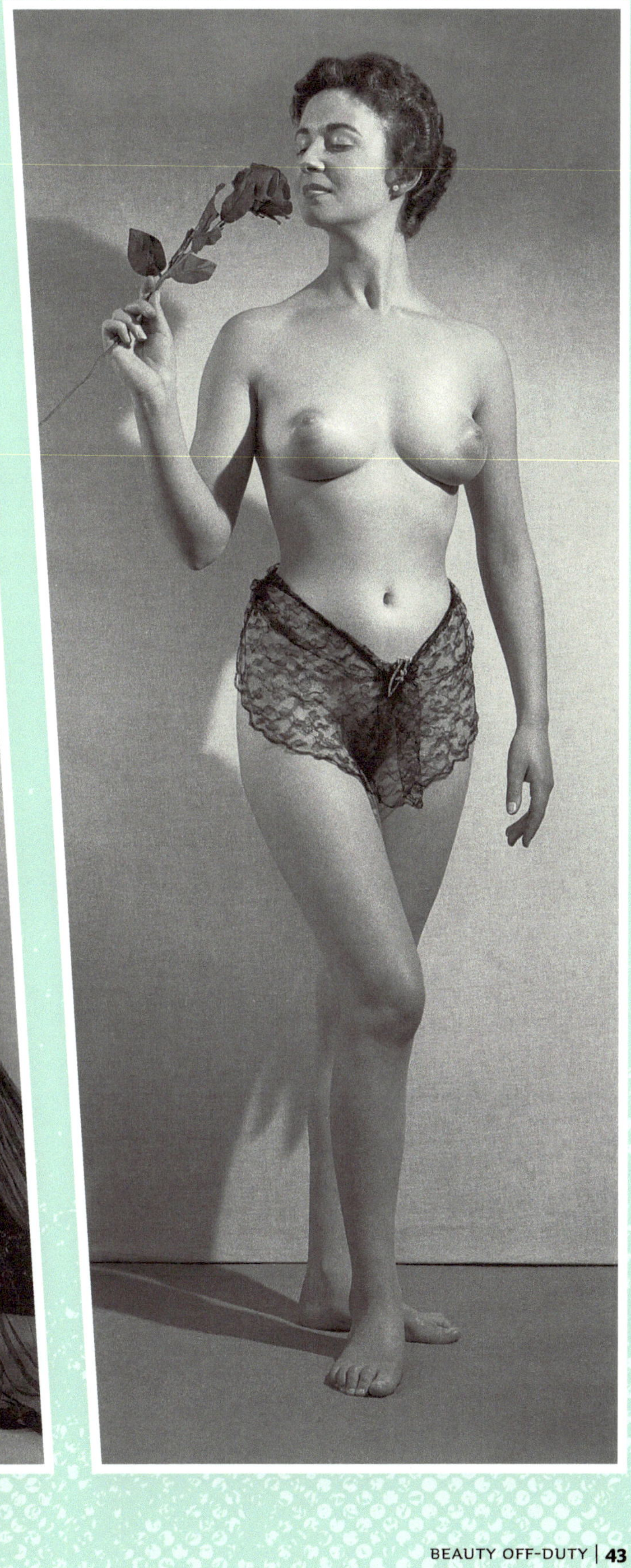

Above left and right: Anita Smith.

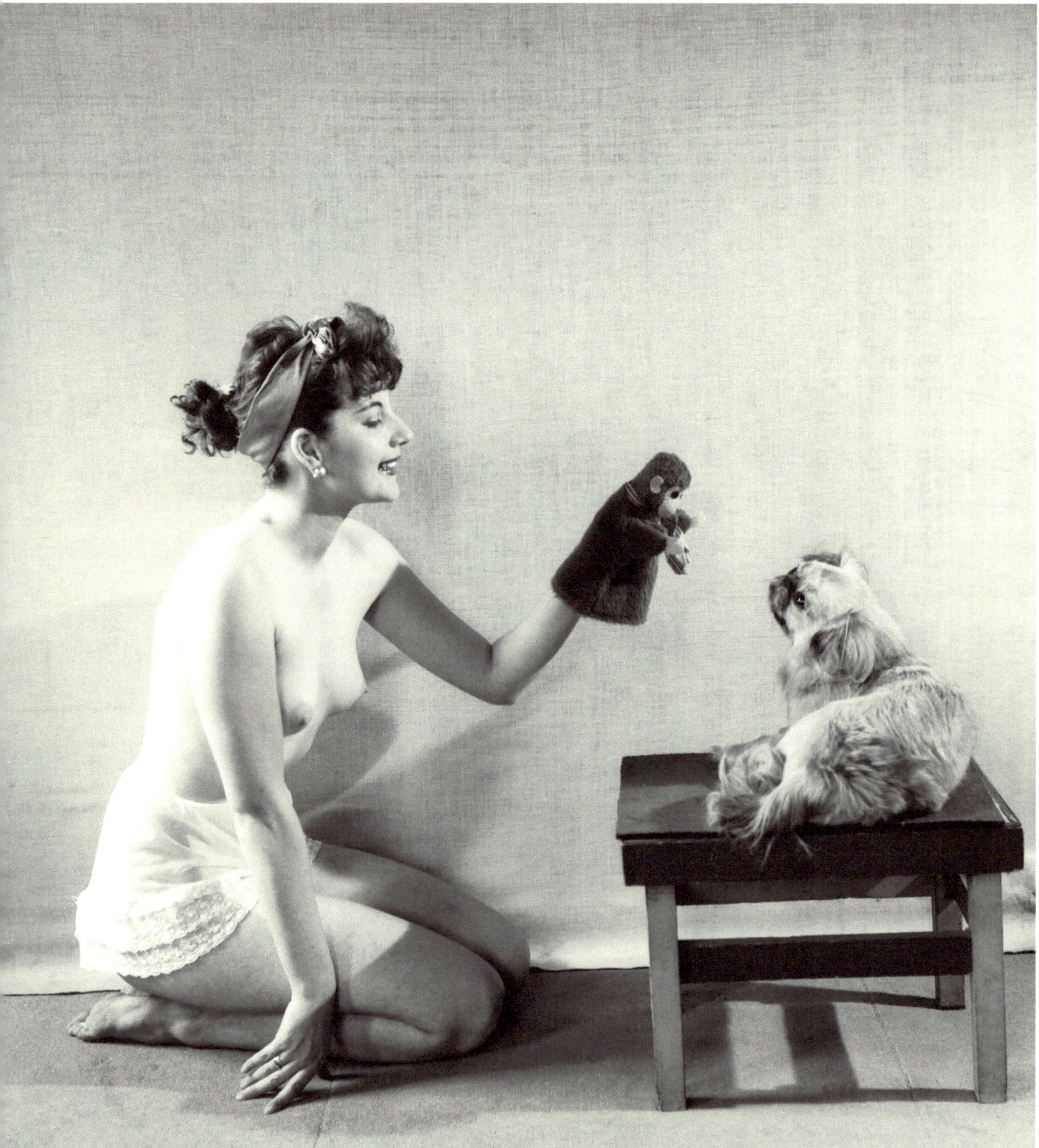

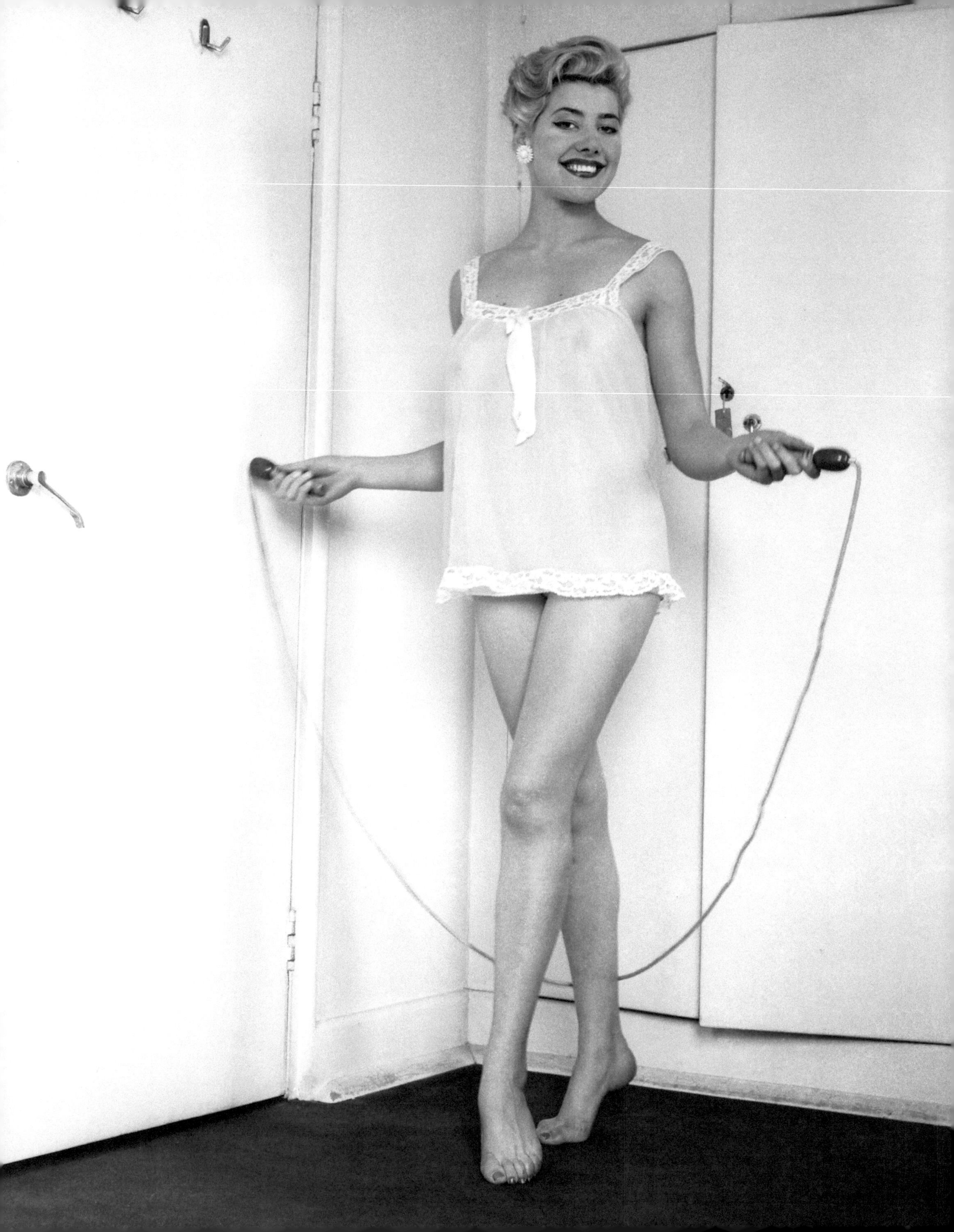

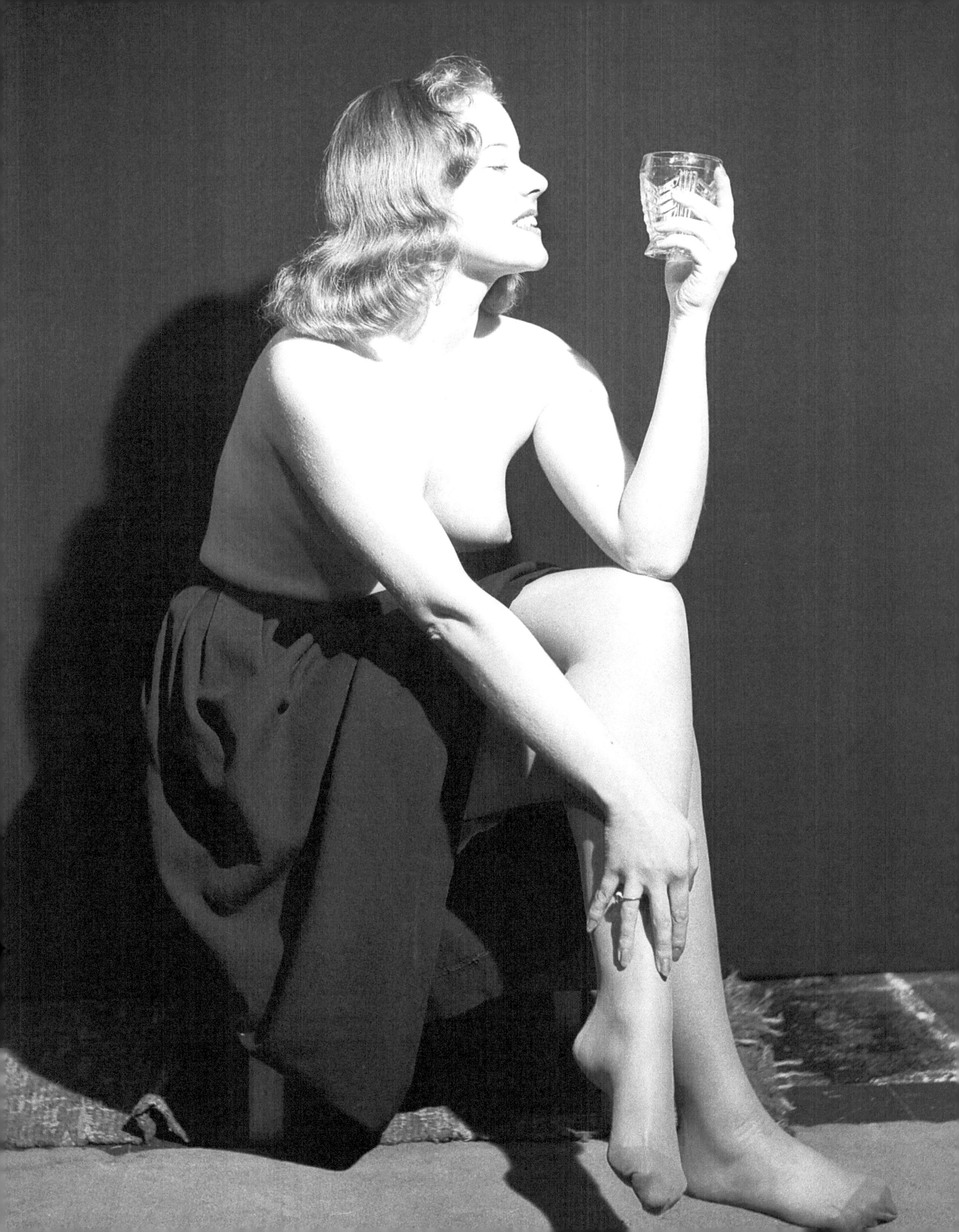

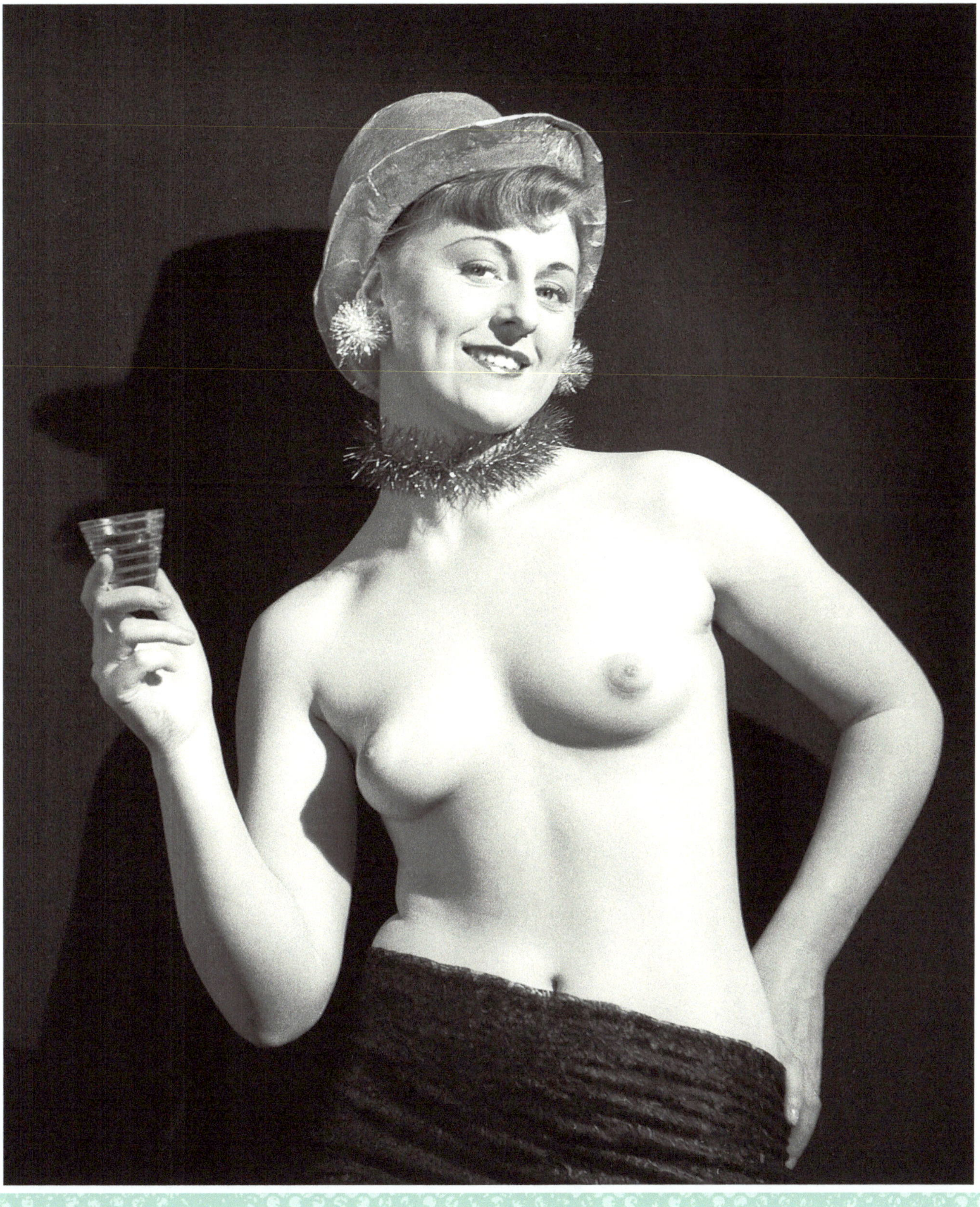

Left: Claudia Gray.

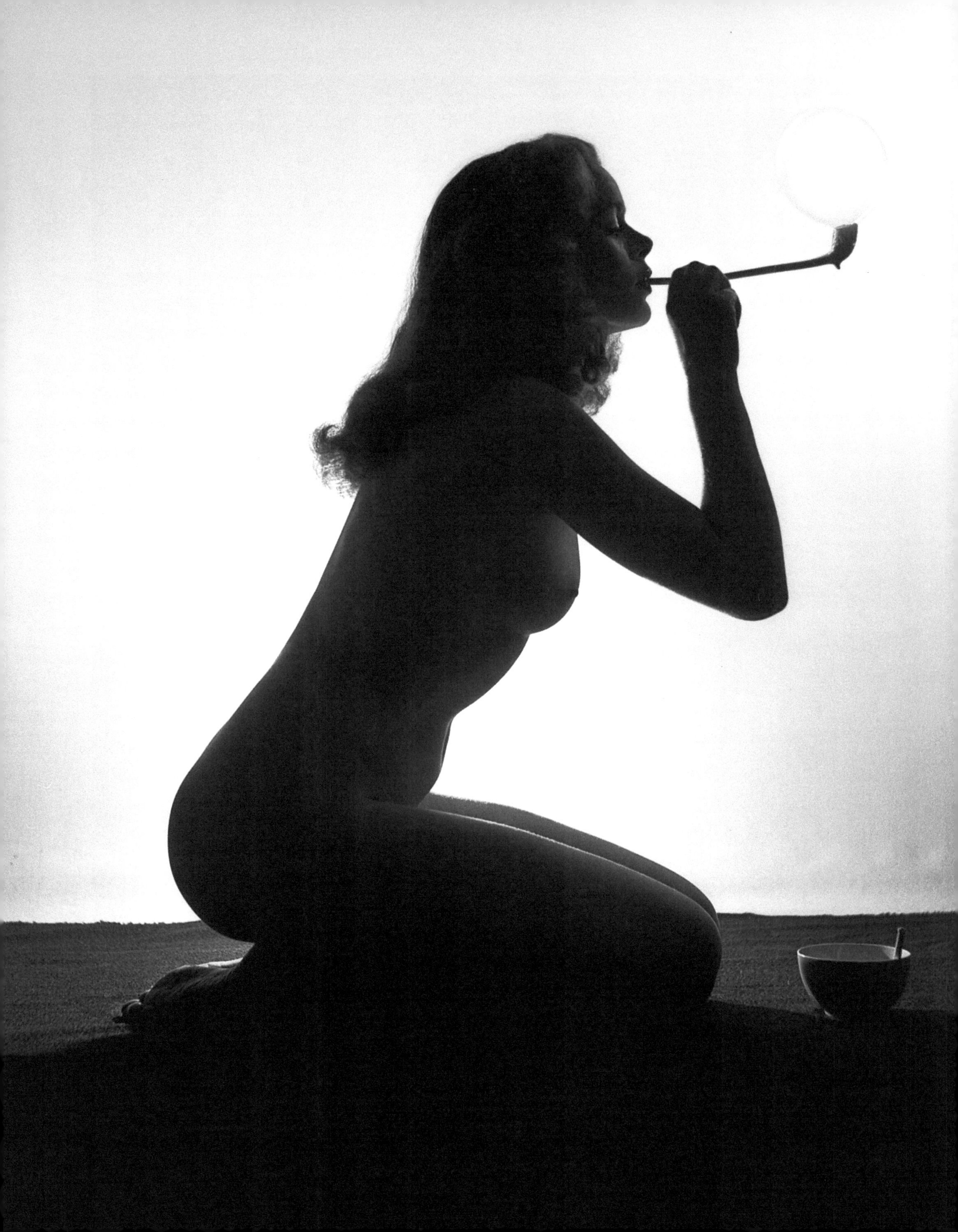

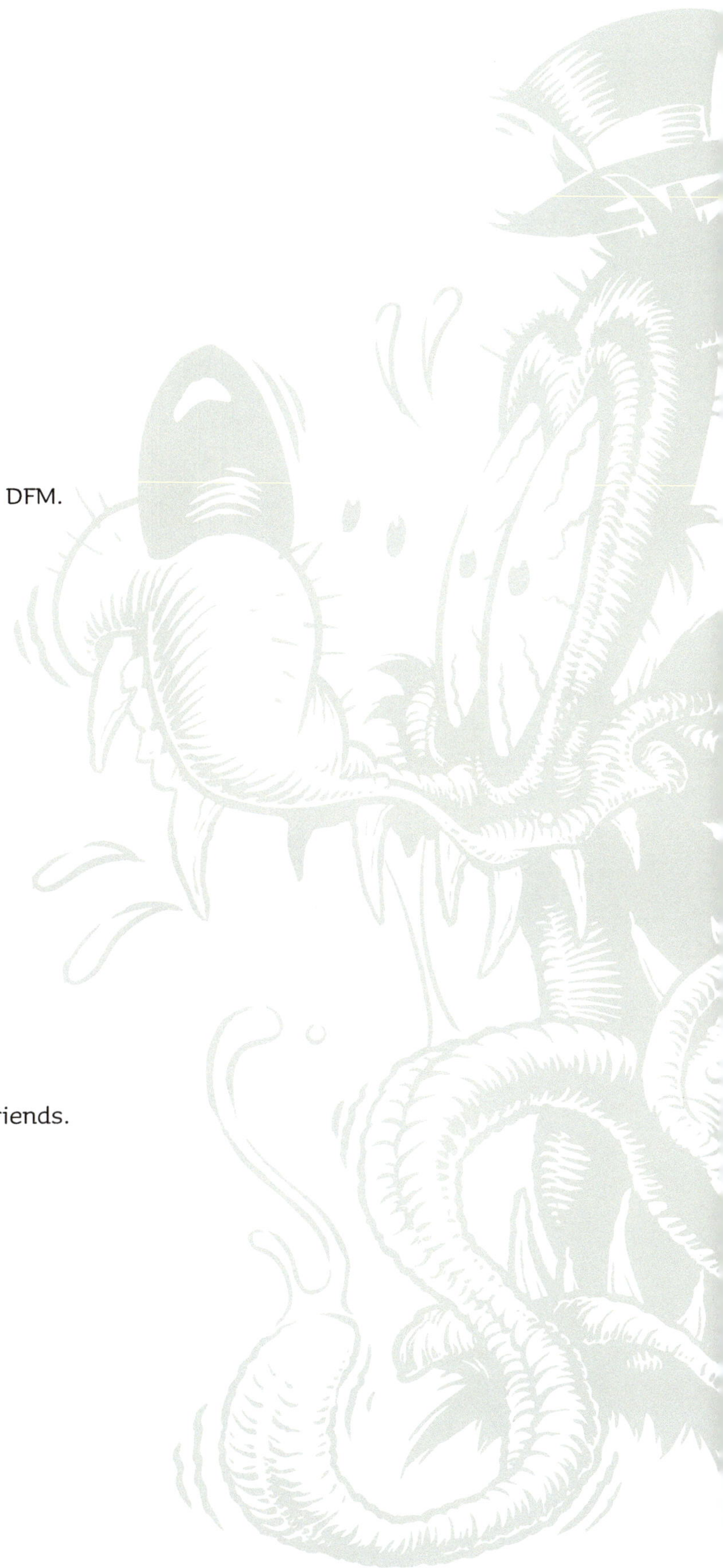

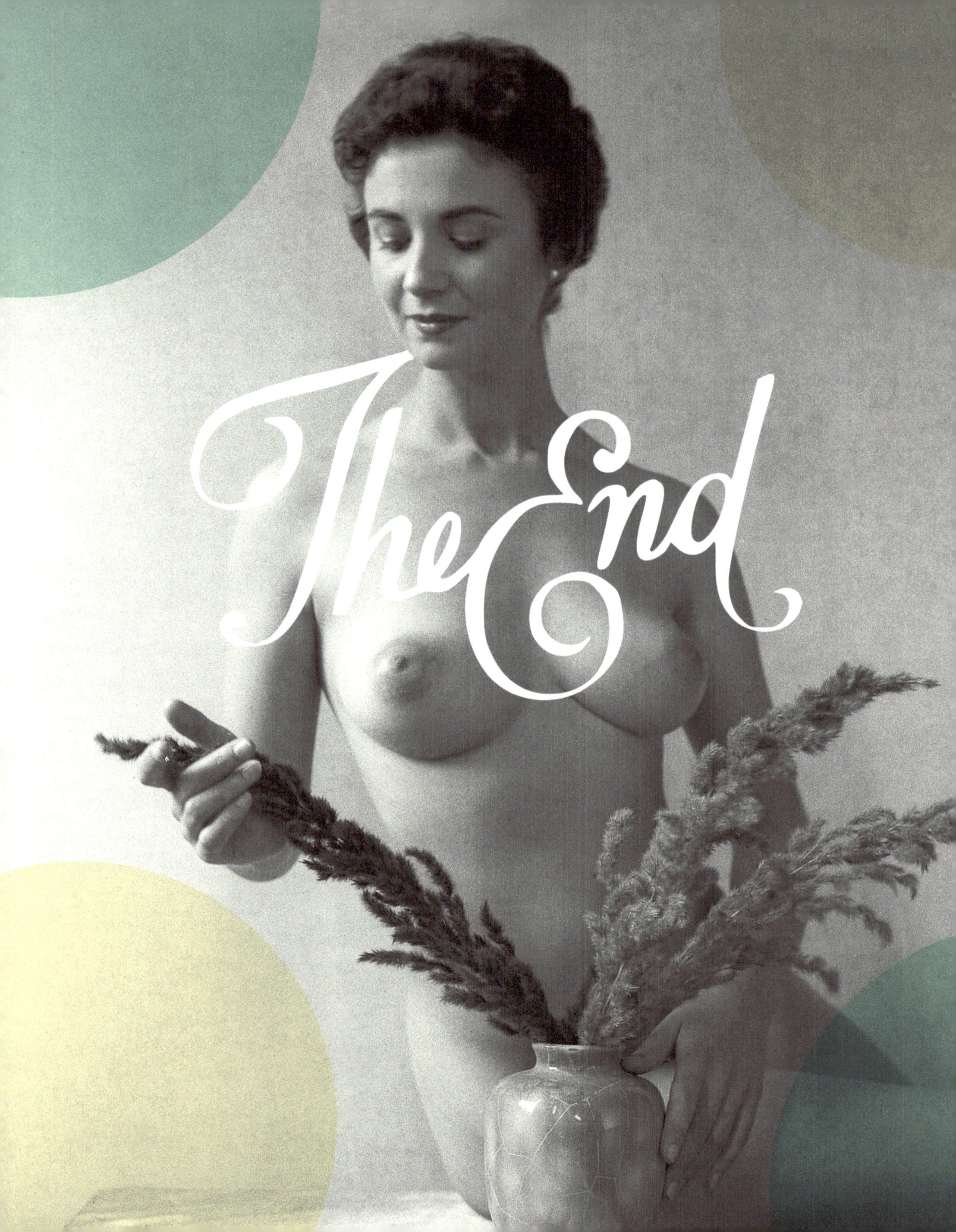
The End

www.ingramcontent.com/pod-product-compliance
Ingram Content Group UK Ltd.
Pitfield, Milton Keynes, MK11 3LW, UK
UKHW061034310726
14089UKWH00010B/230
* 9 7 8 1 9 1 6 2 1 5 1 0 8 *